9/13

Pearls of Patriotism

Pearls of Patriotism

JAY SCHOFIELD

Library of Congress Control Number:		2013902741
ISBN:	Hardcover	978-1-4797-9511-6
	Softcover	978-1-4797-9510-9
	Ebook	978-1-4797-9512-3

This book was printed in the United States of America.

Rev. date: 03/01/2013

To order additional copies of this book, contact:
Xlibris Corporation
1-888-795-4274
www.Xlibris.com
Orders@Xlibris.com
130584

Acknowledgements

I want to thank two people who were extremely helpful in the original editing of the manuscript. The first is Susan Klein and the second is my editor for always and all things, my beautiful wife, Patricia.

This is my first "thank you" for the wonderful people who allowed me to use their stories without which this book would be impossible. Each of these people I have worked with are among the nicest people I have ever known. Sharing their stories has been a highlight in my life of writing.

Dedication

I wish to dedicate this book to our eleven grandchildren who we hope will understand our country's history a little better after reading this book their "Grandpa Scho" dedicated to them.

Their names, in order of birth, are James, Shane, Shivonne, Spencer, Trey, David, Ariana, Shakihra, Aja, Sophia, and Elisa.

Table of Contents

Introduction

The Odds

For every child born in this world only one in forty will be born an American. We Americans are a fortunate few. But it's not enough to be born an American, we should know why this is such a prestigious honor. If we are to appreciate who we are; we must learn our country's history.

As we read this book, I hope more and more people develop an appreciation for just how great it is to be an American. Several contributors for this book are from foreign countries, saw the value of coming to America, and left for its shores.

These are the folks who wanted to *be* Americans, not like some today who simply want to *"live in"* America and get all the benefits without all the work.

Stories Within Stories

As a personal historian, I am privileged to have written many people's life stories, including my own. For this book, I collected "stories within stories" to illustrate how America evolved as told by ordinary citizens including my clients. These "mini-stories" had been passed down through the generations eventually making it to my all-absorbing tape recorder. Following transcription, they ultimately entered my trusty Mac.

While reading these anecdotes, we can begin visualizing people's lives and paint pictures of their ancestors' lifestyles. These visuals show how America was shaped by hard-working people who sacrificed for their families, and by extension, our country. Undoubtedly, their stories provide different perspectives than those in standard history books. They present first-hand observations all placed in chronological order. But many stories didn't make the "cut." Ranging from today's Marine Corps to the Bible's Matthew it is claimed, "Many are called, but, few are chosen." I only selected a few of the hundreds of stories within my books.

These hand-picked family stories begin in our nation's embryonic years and finish in the 21st century.

Clearly, America grew from its immigrants as well as those native born and our sampling of stories originate from my clients' ancestors who had once lived in countries as distant as Ireland, England, Canada, Germany, Italy, and Greece.

First Hand Observations

Americans, especially our youth, symbolize a "Clicker Generation" as countless kids average eight hours a day with "screen time" as they face monitors of either smart phones, televisions, or computers. Many in that age group know precious little of their country's history. Perhaps this book can help ignite a spark of interest in readers of all ages to get involved in the beautiful story of America. Because the book's format is in story form as told by its participants, I'm hoping history can be experienced almost "live" and appear relevant as opposed to the boring memorization of dates and events which seem to typify much of today's taught history.

While teaching, I'd occasionally ask my students simple facts about American history and many were puzzled for the right answer. In jest, I asked the question,

"Do you think American history started with your birthday?"

They laughed but then questioned themselves if I was right. If I planted a seed of introspection in them, I was pleased. Clearly, we have to understand history or we know very little. It's like you are a leaf that's unaware it's part of a tree.

Why Save Stories?

People have been saving stories for thousands of years beginning with the families living in caves as the elders shared stories with the youth. Capturing personal stories has tremendous benefits. I feel everyone should attempt to record their life story. You've got to just get it down and polish it later. When an old person moves on from his earth, they take their remarkable stories to their graves. Another library vanishes. We are all storytellers. It's how we make sense of the world. Even handwritten letters, if saved, can effectively share with their readers the intimate details of daily lives.

With email correspondence, so commonly practiced in today's world, it is just so easy to push the "Delete" button which immediately severs readers from ever reviewing those personal email letters. I often wonder what American historians like the Vineyard's David McCullough would do without personal letters to aid his research for wonderful works such as *John Adams*.

Meeting My Clients

To gain a background of each client and their contributions, I will introduce them to you in their first story and later familiarize you with them later when they re-appear. These folks were a wonderful group of people and I am eager to share their stories since I began writing them in 1996. These stories were either written by me or ones I collaborated on.

Let us begin a new study of American history shared by people like you and me. See their scenes. Hear their words. See why those 1-40 odds of being born an American should be so significant.

The Book's Title

Years ago, back in the 1980s, while coaching high school girls' soccer, I had a wonderful young lady on my team named "Malia." She always wore a string of pearls which I found eye-catching. Malia wore her pearls with everything ranging from sweatshirts to formal wear and looked just great in her trademark accessory.

Those same pearls, when unstrung and carried loosely in a bag, would have little appeal and no function. But when you string them together, they provide an image of beauty with unending unity for the world to see. That is my goal for this book.

I assembled all of these "patriotic pearls" of past writings, these short stories and vignettes, strung them together in this manuscript, and titled it *Pearls of Patriotism*. I thank you, Malia, for your contribution.

The Book's Format

The large chapters are broken up by century beginning with the 1700s.

Each new "pearl of patriotism" begins with a brief introduction about my client and the title of their story. These introductions, along with my editorial notes in the middle, or end of the text will appear in italics to separate my words from those of the client.

Chapter 1

The 1700s

America's Beginnings

Following are a few paragraphs with a thumbnail sketch of early America. It is difficult to compress 150 years into several sentences but here we go . . .

In the early 1600s, emigrants from England arrived on what would be American soil. Why? They wanted economic and religious freedoms. Those who settled in the northeast mainly wanted to choose their own religion. In the south, the English settlements were formed to grow tobacco and eventually cotton. But to increase their earnings, they imported African slaves. As we know, that didn't work all that well.

The newly arrived settlers didn't meet with instant approval with the Native Americans who had lived here long before the English arrived. Yet, several tribes were friendly and helped the newcomers survive the early winters.

War entered the picture in the 1700s once Britain emerged at the top of the world's pig pile for power among European powers. Trying to exert that same power over the colonists, Great Britain started throwing its weight around by taxing them heavily. Those colonists, tired of being pushed around by the very folks they ran from, fought back to achieve those two freedoms I spoke to earlier.

We'll begin our story several decades before the first big war broke out.

The earliest documented family history I have written comes from my own life story titled, "Hey Jay! What's The Story?" This section is based on my ancestors, the maternal Sawins and the paternal Schofields. Each played important roles in forming the foundations of both Canada, our northern

neighbors, and Massachusetts, one of America's original colonies. First, my
maternal ancestors . . .

1754
The Sawins

"My great-great-great-great grandfather, Thomas Sawin, was born in the Boston area almost sixty years before the American Revolution. Renowned as an expert with firearms; he provided food for his growing family with his excellent hunting skills. Along with his prowess in weaponry, he believed in making many young Sawins with his wife (name unknown) who was tens years younger. Thomas first became a father at forty and produced his tenth (and final) Sawin, just thirteen years later. Such constant birthing must have taken its toll on his wife who died just three years later.

"When he wasn't making Sawin children, Thomas fought in the French and Indian War beginning in 1754. Three years later, in 1757, he commanded a detachment of the Natick Military of Garrison Duty in Springfield, MA. That war began when great Britain and France fought for control of the world. Between 1689 and 1773, these two countries went to war four times, the last being the Seven Years' War. The colonists and Great Britain shared a strained relationship suggesting an uncertain future together. With constant military preparation, the colonists stayed focussed on their self-protection. Later, readiness became into play when Thomas Sawin re-enters our story.

1760
The Schofields

"As an early aside, the Schofield name has its origin in "merry old England" meaning "he who lives by the field." But on to the Sawin-Schofield stories . . .

"That same French and Indian War in which Thomas Sawin fought also had a major effect on my paternal ancestors, the Schofields. In 1760, the Brits finally won and took control of North America.

"On a global basis, French power had ended and England ruled most of the world. The treaty signed by both countries granted England the area now known as New Brunswick and Nova Scotia. The long-established French settlements, known as 'Acadia,' were allowed to remain on one condition, they had to take an oath of allegiance to Great Britain. This they refused and thus, they were banned from Nova Scotia. Between 1755 and 1763 British authorities enforced their deportation order, known as the 'Acadian Expulsion.'

"The banished Acadians settled in the colonies to the south with some even extending as far as New Orleans. Great Britain, realizing Nova Scotia's vacated land needed both farmers and fishermen, offered free land grants to farmers, or "planters," from the colonies. Fishermen and farmers got the same amount of land. Newcomers were needed to re-populate the vacated land and also became the first major group of English-speaking immigrants in Canada who did not come directly from Great Britain. Now, on to the Schofields.

"Oliver Cromwell was the rebel ruler of England during England's civil war (1640-1660). He was killed in 1660 and the throne was restored by Charles II. Researchers have suggested that Arthur Schofield, and his brother John, were fighting on the wrong side in that war supporting Oliver Cromwell. At any rate, they were the first Schofields to emigrate from England arrived that same year in 1660.

"One hundred years later, in 1760, Arthur's great-grandson, Arthur left from East Haddam, (now Connecticut) and moved to Nova Scotia where he accepted an offer of free land in exchange for farming his gifted property. This is when our Schofield heritage is traceable back to Nova Scotia and our family history begins.

Nova Scotia Beginnings

"In early June of 1760, my great, great, great, great, great grandfather Arthur Schofield, one of 700 colonists in forty ships, sailed up the Gaspereau River to the town of Horton, Nova Scotia to claim his "free" land. They set up a little community of tents and temporary shelters. These planters were given either a half share (200 acres) for a single person, a full share (400 acres), or a share-and-a-half (600 acres) of land to develop as they wished. The new planters lived close to their farm land to protect it from marauding Indians. When hostilities lessened, and travel became safer, they moved back to the village of Horton, now called Wolfville.

"The land was considered almost worthless in terms of planting anything but the Schofields were a determined lot. Some of the Schofields did so well at farming their neighbors accused them of gaining their riches from discovering some of the pirate treasures which tradition says lie buried all along the southwest coast of Nova Scotia.

1763
The Schofield Family Begins in Nova Scotia

"Three years later, at 28, Arthur married Jermina Coldwell. He seemed so taken with his new wife that he neglected to collect the King's reward of 50 pounds (around $250, a large sum of money in those days) for the first marriage in Nova Scotia having partners of English descent. Evidently, the desirable Jemina's value exceeded the $250 reward many times over.

1775
The American War of Independence

"Twelve years later, after a series of events, the Thirteen Colonies and the British each declared war. But the war's names differed. Britain named it the 'American Revolutionary War' while the colonists called it the 'American War of Independence'

"The war, triggered in part, by The Boston Tea Party began on April 19, 1775, with the battles in Lexington and Concord. It was. The British sent a regiment to confiscate arms and ammunition from some local 'revolutionaries.' The colonists, on their home turf, were determined they'd had enough from England with their relentless waves of taxes and oppression. In all-out battle, Britain's so called "elite "troops fared poorly against the local militia or 'Minutemen.' Reinforcements with their primitive weapons arrived to increase the British casualties. The British Army retreated to Boston after taking heavy losses. The colonists must have been a brave lot and I'm proud to say our very own Thomas Sawin, with sons, Thomas and Moses, served in the local militia.

"The Schofields helped make Nova Scotia what it is today and the Sawins were equally instrumental in establishing Massachusetts and ultimately our United States. I'm proud to know my blood has coursed through the veins of both heritages."

May, 1775
Revolutionary War—Aboard the *Falcon*

The first person we meet in telling our stories is a woman named Eugenia "Gene" Seamans. Her book, titled "Light & Love" was completed in 2003. This wonderful woman captured, then related to me, her ancestors' contributions toward building America. We combined her quotes with my parallel research to round out dates and names and get a glimpse of America's early years. I loved interviewing her and so appreciate all she provided.

Remember that just two years before this date the Boston Tea Party erupted as an act of revolt against the British and their tax on tea coming into the colonies. England felt they had the right to impose this tax because their funds were low following their efforts to protect us from the French.

Eugenia Seamans' great-great-grandfather, Elisha Ayer, is the key figure in this story which begins with privateering. She tells her story . . .

"Privateering began when the colonists hired privately-owned ships and crews to fight during wartime. The colonists improvised this emergency measure to contend with England's mighty naval strength. Once the Second Continental Congress authorized their use, these private ships played major roles in the American Revolution. Using these makeshift battle vessels, the colonists captured over 600 British ships. Let's examine one such colonist/privateer, Mrs. Seaman's ancestor, Elisha Ayer.

"At 17, as half owner of the privateering ship *Falcon*, Mr. Ayer, from Stonington, Connecticut, was aboard the two-masted schooner under command of Captain Joseph Breed. They were engaged in coastal trade in New England waters when a large British man-of-war battle ship approached them. The colonists, noting the potential fighting power in the ship's size, crew, and weapons, had no choice but to surrender. Fighting would have been useless. Once captured, the British officers forced three of the *Falcon's* shipmates, to join their navy with promises to spare their lives and eventually free them. Once again underway, the British headed north toward Canada as they feared local counterattacks from vengeful privateering vessel.

"Young Mr. Ayer was one of the three captured colonists. The other two captives were Captain Breed and an unknown sailor. None of the three captive, but determined patriots believed their captors' promise of freedom. En route to Canada, they quietly discussed escape plans.

Escape!

"One night, shortly after their arrival in Quebec, the three colonists silently slipped over the side from the anchored man-of-war. The moonless night hid them well and the ocean's slight chop masked their slow motion "dog-paddling" efforts as they made their way quietly to shore, about three miles away. No words or splashes were needed to reach the shore.

"They covered that first mile noiselessly under great discomfort. One of the men became totally exhausted. He wanted to quit and die a free man. But, Mr. Ayer and the other man would hear none of it as they put the tired swimmer between them. With a fierce determination to live, despite the linked swimming formation, they struggled toward land. When they were within a mile of shore, noise erupted back on the ship when their escape became apparent. British rowboats, were immediately dispatched to find the three swimmers. Although they came close to the men several times, each ducked underwater almost as if on cue as boats passed above them.

"Both the escapees and the Brits needed perfect silence. The three men knew that after one boat passed them, they had to be wary of the next approaching boat. These evasive tactics continued as the men slowly, and silently, made their way toward the shoreline's dim silhouette.

"After reaching shore, they quietly approached a nearby swamp as the rowboat pulled up on shore minutes behind them. With the British voices close by, the men waded cautiously into the swamp and found individual hiding places. With no idea what wildlife lived in the water, the exhausted swimmers stayed still and silent. Putting cold, fatigue and hunger behind them, they watched their former captors comb the swamp throughout that night and all of the next day. They remained hidden there with its unknown fellow inhabitants until the British gave up and rowed back to their ship. The three had survived their initial hurdle.

"Finding no escapees, the ship left the area at sunrise the following day. Relieved, Elisha Ayer and the other two men needed a new strategy to satisfy their two immediate needs: food, then freedom. They combined their soaked money, hired an old man to bring them food, and asked him to contact any nearby friendly ship. They hoped the stranger could persuade its captain to take them aboard. Each man was desperate for a return to the colonies. Their hired man was successful on both counts.

"The three fugitives were eventually picked up by a Scottish vessel which was heading east. Once in Halifax, Nova Scotia, they again jumped ship and stole a small sailboat which anchored in a bay. Once aboard, they set a southerly course toward Boston.

"On their journey home, they caught some codfish (...hence the naming of Cape Cod because of all the codfish in the area.) which they boiled and ate. To stave off their increasing thirst, they drank the same water in which they had cooked the codfish. Within two months, they returned safely to the colonies and then on to their respective home towns.

"Back in Connecticut, Mr. Ayer was met with shock and seen as a returning hero. The sad story of his original capture had reached his home town within days and, after him missing for two months, they considered him dead. An old schoolmate, upon seeing him, thought he was a ghost until a conversation proved otherwise. His life began anew."

We must remember that the flame of independence was already burning brightly in the colonists' hearts and America had yet to be born. Mr. Ayer and friends knew what was right for their fledgling country and that Great Britain's tyranny had gone too far.

1782
War Ends, America is Born

After the war was over and the British decided to leave us to our own devices, Massachusetts wrote their own Constitution of the Commonwealth of Massachusetts. Written by John Adams, Samuel Adams, and James Bowdoin, it made Massachusetts a free and sovereign state.

Other co-signers of America's (and the world's) oldest functioning constitution were three of our afore-mentioned ancestors, the Sawins: Thomas and his two sons, Moses and Thomas Jr.

In 1783, Great Britain and the colonists signed The Treaty of Paris which ended the war. British folks agreed that the colonists had earned the right to go it alone. Following the Revolutionary War, the available states agreed to form a national government with a constitutional convention in 1787. There, they decided that the highly successful General George Washington would be their president. They figured he held our Continental Army together so who better to lead the country?

We became the United States as we expanded to the west and south gradually adding more states. But in the process of expansion, we bothered quite a few Native Indians. Following some questionably legal land titles after trading with some of the chiefs, others were not thrilled with the notion they were losing their tribal lands. Some powerful Indian leaders formed alliances with other tribes and were backed by our former foe, the British. They wanted to stop our western expansion.

Chapter 2

The 1800s

America began to grow. Folks from other countries noticed that this country could provide them a new start if they could reach our shores. But those trips across the ocean dangerous and expensive. One of the largest populations to immigrate here were the Irish. They moved here in the mid-1800s because many were starving due to the Great Famine, a "potato rot" which ignited a mass migration. By 1840, one of every two immigrants to America were Irish.

With the help of a recent memoirs client, Dianna Gantt, in her tentatively titled book "I Gantt Believe Life Is This Good" we will describe what an immigrant's passage was like as she relates the story of John Walsh, her great-great-grandfather, as he came from Ireland.

1853
Immigration—John Lawrence Walsh

"On December 18, 1842, in Saxony, Germany, a woman named Catherine Barbara Mcduvott gave birth to a baby boy, John Lawrence Walsh. As his great-great-granddaughter, I have loved tracing his travels, including their uncertainties.

"This boy somehow moved to Ireland from Germany sometime before he was eleven years old. That explained why he could speak English when he arrived in America.

"Records show he left Ireland, traveled to England, and immigrated to America in 1853. There is a strong likelihood he moved to America because Ireland was then in such bad shape. In the middle 1800s, Ireland's Great Famine brought many deaths to Irish of all ages. Between 1845 and 1852 Ireland lost one quarter of its population which devastated the country. Along with those one million deaths, another million emigrated from Ireland's shores seeking better lives in lands with ample food, work, and freedom of disease.

"Shortly after arriving in England from Ireland, eleven-year-old John Lawrence Walsh made a decision. Wanting to emigrate to America, he somehow learned a ship named *Northern Light* was scheduled to cross the Atlantic from Liverpool. With no money, there was no choice for young John except to sneak aboard as a stowaway. He wanted to reach America as so many Europeans raved about its opportunities for work and food, both of which Ireland lacked. As he thought of his upcoming trip, the facts that must must have weighed heavily on his eleven-year-old mind was that he was still learning English, had neither family or friends in a new country, all with no money. What courage he must have had!

"He must have studied the ship with an eye on the cargo being loaded up the ramps and hatched a plan to sneak aboard. Part of the cargo, however, included cows. Young John was likely unaware that most European cows had, at the time, the highly contagious 'Cattle Plague.' The world's few healthy cows were much in demand and America was importing them. The *Northern Light* had apparently been contracted to transport some of these few healthy cows across the Atlantic. Accordingly, John probably figured if he was to hide on this ship, the cows would be his traveling companions.

"Finally, the ship's date of departure, January 19, 1853, had arrived and John made his move likely walking up the ramp hoping to appear he belonged. After somehow slipping through the ship' security cracks, my stowaway ancestor found his way to the ship's hold in search of a secure hiding place. He must have been shocked to see the cows being herded in the same direction! His hopes of relative comfort must have been dashed once he realized these cows would be his sleep mates. I can't imagine bedding down each night in a manger with the cattle's constant "mooing" and accompanying smells. He must have survived this tortuous and lengthy transatlantic journey on scraps of food he could somehow scrounge. There was little, if any, conversation with other travelers. He had one goal: to reach America.

"John's ship wasn't necessarily bound for America's nearest cities, like New York or Boston, as he expected. Records show the *Northern Light* instead hugged the American coastline all the way to New Orleans, Louisiana, a much prolonged journey. But what joy he must have experienced once he walked off that ship's gangplank, viewed a new continent for the first time, and deeply breathed in clean American air. But he soon experienced an unwelcome event.

"Within six months of his arrival, he discovered New Orleans was facing a full-scale epidemic of yellow fever that killed 11,000 people in one summer. Thankfully, he survived. Perhaps it was due to the built-up immunity he'd acquired sleeping with those cows and whatever filth they brought! My maternal family history in America had begun. I am so proud of what he achieved and thankful I must have inherited some of his genes for success."

1862
Civil War

The battles and wars during the early 1800s almost served as "warm-ups" for what was to be the single war which killed the most Americans—our Civil War. During these wars a fight of words was simmering between the North who opposed slavery and the South who needed slaves to keep their crops growing and selling.

The Mason-Dixon line was formed saying that any state to the north accepted slavery would not be allowed in the union. The "North" and the "South" were established.

Soon, our country was even further divided with the theory of "nullification" which meant that states could decide for themselves which federal laws they chose to follow.

Hard to believe, but an 1857 Supreme Court decision stated that slaves had no more rights than mules! Now that bothered the North and only fired up their anti-slavery attitudes all the more. It was just a matter of time.

Three years later, Abe Lincoln won the presidency which, in turn, fired up the South. They figured it was time to leave the Union.

Early in 1861, our Civil War began. It was an ongoing battle to preserve the Union, President Lincoln's primary goal.

We have several stories shared by my former clients which well describe the horrors of this period in our country's fabled history. The Civil War was a sad time in America as it became the deadliest in our history causing over 600,000 soldiers' deaths. Yes, it ended slavery. Yes, it restored the Union. And finally, yes, it strengthened the role of the federal government. But, pitting brother against brother and family against family was costly in so many ways.

We are staying in the Civil War era for yet another account of Dianna Gantt's ancestor, John Lawrence Walsh. We met earlier when he immigrated from Ireland and landed unexpectedly in New Orleans where he avoided the epidemic of yellow fever, Dianna Gantt in her tentatively titled book ("I Gantt Believe Life is This Good") continues her story below.

1861
Camp Moore, Louisiana

"I don't know what happened to him between his arrival in 1853 and the beginning of the Civil War in 1861. My guess is he may have worked as a laborer while improving his English. Shortly after the war started, my great-great-grandfather, at nineteen, must have fallen in love with his new country, empathized with the southern cause, and signed up to fight for the South.

"In 1901, his application for a military pension filed in McDowell County, North Carolina, gave pertinent details: John Lawrence Walsh joined Co. K, 6th Regiment of the Louisiana Infantry in April, 1861, at Camp Moore, Louisiana. When enlisting, he was asked his place of birth to which he responded 'Ireland.' He completed it listing his occupation as 'laborer' and his current home as 'New Orleans.' Why would he state 'Ireland' when, as family history suggests, he was born in Germany? A possible explanation follows.

"German men who left their homeland in the middle 1800s seldom mentioned their German backgrounds or even their family name. Why? Because the German military had been involved in various skirmishes for years and its citizens were tired of war. Fathers, being military veterans, rather than risk their sons being drafted left the country never to return. Sadly, once their new lives had begun in other countries such as America, they were reluctant to reveal their German heritage. They feared a forcible return to Germany to either serve its army or face severe punishment. These men, possibly seen as deserters, also sought to avoid governmental retribution inflicted on remaining family members still living in Germany. Stories were told of unsuspecting family members, back home, being harassed. Maybe John Lawrence Walsh didn't want to take any chances down the line being considered a German as his English had improved sufficiently to overcome his native German accent. At any rate, off he went to fight for the South.

"Part of his soldiering campaign brought him to Gaines' Mill, VA, the site of an early Civil War battle against Union forces. John Walsh fought under the leadership of General Robert E. Lee against those Union forces led by Brig. General Fitz John Porter. On that afternoon of June 27, 1862, the North held strong while inflicting heavy casualties on the attacking Confederates. At dusk, the Confederates counterattacked Porter's forces and drove them back toward a nearby river. Under fire that night, the Federal forces retreated back across the river, but the southerners had lost their chance. They were too disorganized to encircle the retreating Union forces and finish them off. Clearly, that Union defeat at Gaines' Mill stopped their intended advance to capture Richmond, the capital of the Confederate States of America.

"The northern forces numbered just 34,000 participants of which almost 7,000 were killed and 3,000 were wounded. On the other hand, the South included 57,000 soldiers, lost 8,000 and the wounded numbered just over 6,000. One of those wounded southern boys was my ancestor, John Lawrence Walsh.

"He received a severe wound in his right ankle which required extensive healing. Hopeful of full recovery, he spent time in Richmond's Camp Winder Hospital. Sadly, the full healing process never happened leaving him with a lifelong limp. The good news is, although he had no friends back in New Orleans, he met a man named F. M. Stepp, the hospital's ward master. These two young veterans became close friends, were discharged together, and somehow made their way back to Mr. Stepp's home town of Old Fort, McDowell County, North Carolina. Twenty-year-old John Walsh eventually settled in as a farmer in a nearby small town named Nick's Creek Community located in Marion, NC.

"Within six years, John met a woman named Ruth Anor Krause. Their first conversation couldn't have lasted too long before they realized they were both German immigrants. It was learned her father, Charles F. Krause, was born in Germany but little more is known of him. She came to New York City from 'Abroad' so I assume she was also from Germany.

"John and Ruth were married December 31, 1868. He had just turned twenty-six, she was nineteen.

"His attraction to her must have been powerful as she was bald from getting typhoid fever as a young girl during the Civil War. For the rest of her life, 'Mama Dutch,' as she was affectionately known, always covered her head."

Our next entry into the 1800s is with a woman named Dorothea Looney. She and I collaborated on her book which she titled simply, 'Our Story,' written in 2002. Dorothea brings the reader some great insight into the Civil War through one of her ancestors, James Doherty. His story was passed to his family members and then carried down through the years. This is the real thing, war as we can't imagine it. Dorothea's account of James is fascinating . . .

The Civil War
1861

"I don't know what sort of job James had before the war; he may have worked in a factory. That time period was at the beginning of the Industrial Revolution and I believe there must have been some sort of industry in town. It could have been a saw mill, small textile plant, or a foundry which made castings from molten metal.

"Whatever his job, he soon had another one as a soldier in the Union Army. This came about when our lad, a new citizen of the United States, while primed with patriotic fervor and good whiskey, volunteered to serve. He was in the local tavern with his buddies and this move seemed a great idea. But, when he went home and had to explain it to his wife, it didn't seem such a wise plan. His wife felt that, although he would undoubtedly be of great service to his country, he would be of immeasurably more use to his wife and daughters at home.

"Even though James had officially enlisted, there was still a way out. At that time, if you didn't want to fulfill your promise to enlist, you could pay somebody else to go for you. The price for the 'bounty' as it was called, had reached $300 which, for them, was an enormous sum of money. They somehow managed to raise the money, I shudder to think how. They paid another man to go for him but that creature took their money and 'jumped the bounty.' In other words, he crossed the border into Canada with the $300. James had no alternative but to follow through on his original enlistment.

"So, on the twenty-sixth of June 1862, James Doherty was mustered into the service of the United States as a private in Company D, Ninth Regiment Infantry, New Hampshire Volunteers, for a period of three years.

September 16-18, 1862
News From The Front

"For what happened next, we have two sources of information: The History of the Ninth New Hampshire and James's own letters. Since James couldn't read, or write, his letters were written for him by his fellow soldiers. The regimental history indicates that the Ninth fought first at Antietam, Maryland, on September 16-18th, 1862. Following this battle, they marched West through Kentucky while heading for Vicksburg, Mississippi. Once they arrived, they were told the battle had been already fought, so they turned right around and headed back east.

"During this easterly march, they joined forces with General Grant's Army of the Potomac. They then fought through Virginia, notably in the battle at The Wilderness, and later in Spottsylvania in 1864. It was at Spottsylvania, a particularly brutal encounter where 17,000 men were lost, that James' Ninth Regiment Infantry got the worst assignment of all. The battle of Spottsylvania Courthouse was fought at very close range for three days. To take the area, a strategic triangle was formed, subsequently named the 'Bloody Triangle,' and this is where the Ninth was sent. There, they took enormous causalities. That's the official record from the sources of history.

James' Letters Home

"Fortunately, we have James' letters home which provide a more personal account of his days as a soldier. His letters all began according to the polite formula of the day.

'Dear Wife,

This letter leaves me in the best of health and I hope it finds you in the same.'

"The military censors reading letters home were also active in those days. Instead of the ink-outs used in World War II, they used scissors and just cut out whole words, especially anything about a soldier's location. I do remember one letter marked 'Somewhere in Tennessee.' I suppose that was sufficiently vague to get by. My overall impression of his letters was that they sounded like soldiers' letters anywhere, anytime.

"We (her sisters, Rita, and Michie,) were reading these letters about the time of World War II and I believe we could all claim some familiarity with soldiers' letters. The recurrent themes were 1) 'The food was awful.' and 2) 'It was about time I got a furlough!' James had a particular grievance on this last point after he met his cousin, Mike Doherty, of the Fifth Maine. Mike told James that although he hadn't been in as long as James, he had already received a furlough.

"In general, he talked about the circumstances in the camps and the condition of the contents of the packages his wife sent him. He was very upset that the fruit cake was wormy but the crackers arrived in great shape. He suggested that she not send any more fruit cake. The only other remark he made, which I remember, was his speaking of seeing 'a woman shopping who had a young black lad following her and carrying her packages.' He thought this was a "very convenient arrangement and regretted he couldn't send her (his wife) a little black boy of her own. Our lad did not sound like an abolitionist."

May 12, 1864
James Is Wounded

"It was at the battle of Spottsylvania Courthouse that James was wounded. The record reads ' . . . wounded May 12th, 1864, at Spottsylvania, Virginia. Died of wounds May 14th, Fredericksburg, Virginia.'

"There was, of course, more to it than that. The family was told that he had been shot in the leg. Considering the primitive medical care at that time, a Minie' ball in the leg was usually a fatal injury. There were no antibiotics so the subsequent infection killed them fast. His going from Spottsylvania in central Virginia to the hospital in Fredericksburg, VA, is the interesting part of the story. After he was wounded in the leg, he couldn't get up to return back to the Union lines. James was lying on the battlefield in Confederate territory as night fell. At that time, a truce was observed as each side gathered up their wounded comrades. But, there were no Yankee soldiers in the area to pick him up and carry him back to friendly lines.

"There were Confederate soldiers all around him and, knowing he couldn't expect much, nevertheless asked a Confederate soldier for a drink of water. The soldier replied with a question:

"What's your name?

"When James told him his name was 'Doherty' the Confederate soldier replied: 'I wouldn't do anything for you but my name is Doherty too!'

"With that, the soldier not only gave him water but picked him up and carried him near the Union lines where he was later picked up by his own men and brought to a hospital. Shortly after, he died in that same hospital, rather than on the battlefield. James had the opportunity to share this story with fellow soldiers who wrote back to his family members of the incident."

Spring of 1864
The White House

As an observer, I found it welcoming that, despite the vast differences between the two soldiers, both were still Americans and treated each other with respect.

The next entry comes from Mrs. Gene Seamans, in her book, "Light & Love." You may remember, her Great-Great-Grandfather Ayer was the privateer who escaped from the British in Canada. This hero's grandson, Frederick Ayer, enters our story with an in-depth account of President Lincoln during the heavy stressful times while he was coping with the Civil War as it raged. Gene described that meeting below.

"It was hot. President Lincoln, feeling the heat, had rolled up his sleeves, removed his tie, and unbuttoned his vest. Perspiration had so soaked his shirt that its collar lay flat on his shoulders. He had just completed his morning's work in the office except for one more appointment with five businessmen. He was not excited about more business than what he already had to deal with. There was a knock at the door and an aide admitted them.

"As the five men entered the room, the president stood up. He looked terribly tired, extremely bored, almost lifeless. The Civil War was tearing the country apart and he seemed to bear the weight of each battle on his shoulders. His facial expression and body language both reflected the enormous stress. President Lincoln had learned to expect from such men either scathing criticism or special favors. One of the men, Mr. Frederick Ayer, had been chosen as the group's spokesman. He was forty-two at the time and, years later, would become my grandfather.

"He first introduced himself to the president and then each of the other four gentleman. My grandfather got right to the point:

'Mr. President, we have called only to pay our respects to our President. None of us has a favor to ask . . . not even a country post office.'

"President Lincoln's expression changed abruptly. It showed new life. Even relief. With a smile, he stepped toward Mr. Ayer with both hands leading the way. It seemed an embrace was possible. Instead, the President took both of Mr. Ayer's hands and shook them vigorously. He spoke with sincerity:

'Gentlemen, I am glad to see you. You are the first men I have seen since I have been president who didn't want something!'

"A brief conversation followed and the men said their good-byes. The President, punctuated their visit's ending with more energetic handshakes. Everyone benefitted from the brief and simple meeting. The five men left the office and never saw their President again.

"My Grandfather Ayer, whom I never knew, had wisdom, understanding and appreciated people, especially his family."

Rosalie Powell, in her life story yet to be titled, spoke of her ancestors during the Civil War.

1863
End of Civil War

My father told us stories about their grandparents, aunts, and uncles. One involved my Grandfather Reed who, along with Grandfather Humphrey, served in the Civil War fighting as Confederate soldiers from Arkansas. Following the war, Grandfather Reed received his honorable discharge in Texas, a long way from home.

He had little in the way of personal belongings but, what he did have, was placed in an old wooden bucket. He carried that bucket during his long walk home, a journey of hundreds of miles, back to Clarksville, Arkansas. He made it safely home while keeping his bucket's limited life possessions intact. For years, the Reed descendants treasured that old bucket as a remembrance of this man's perseverance.

1864
General Schofield

Before leaving the Civil War era, one of our Schofield ancestors tracing back one hundred years earlier was named John McAllister Schofield, who became a West Point graduate following a brief stint as a civil engineer and land surveyor.

This soldier went on to distinguish himself as one of President Lincoln's leading Civil War Union generals. As an officer, he awarded the first Congressional Medal of Honor to a black soldier. Years later, President Teddy Roosevelt named Hawaii's Schofield Barracks after him.

To continue on with the Schofields and their connection with American history, I want to introduce the reader to my paternal grandfather, James Weston Schofield as told in my memoir "Hey, Jay! What's The Story?" I remember a few things about him but research and oral history provide the bulk of his inspirational story.

"Born in 1884, he was the first son and second oldest child, of what would later number sixteen children. But today's 'Big Brother Privileges' were hardly privileges back then. Older children, like James 'Jim' Schofield, were required to work outside their home to help feed his younger brothers and sisters.

"Sixteen mouths to feed, bodies to clothe, and a shortage of beds, called for massive changes. One way to solve such critical shortages demanded some of the older children leave home despite their tender ages. Older siblings were often 'indentured' out to other families to help them run their farms. Perhaps the term 'farmed out' had its origins in this common practice.

"Farms, forever labor-intensive, knew no age boundaries in their 'hiring practices.' 'Cheap labor' meant 'child labor' most of which was done by boys. Yet in that same setting, girls were also farmed out to help housewives care for their homes and young children. Given that the Schofield family needed fewer growling stomachs, more living space and cash, changes was called for. Ten-year-old James, became 'indentured' to another farming family which had either fewer children (or no children) to help with chores.

"Young Jim Schofield (barely Little League baseball age in today's world) lived and worked on a farm somewhere in Gaspereau, Nova Scotia, to improve his family's life back home. The seeds of sacrifice for family were sown early in his life and would be nurtured all his days.

"His jobs started early in the morning. Before the rising sun, the household's mother roused young Jim from bed two hours before breakfast. Before his own hunger could be satisfied, he had fed and cared for the farm's livestock including its horses, cattle, sheep, pigs and chickens. That alone would be a daunting task fueled on an empty stomach for any man, let alone a growing boy. There was no complaining, however, as such efforts were expected, just like the animals expected their food early in the day. With no other comparison, young Jim likely felt his life was a normal life. Perhaps he assumed every boy his age lived the same life he did.

"Fireplaces, in those cold Nova Scotia winters, remained the only source of heat and Jim's labors extended to providing that fuel. Following his first meal, he split wood, filled up the farm's wood boxes, then emptied ashes from all the stoves and fireplaces. Then, continued animal care occupied his day until he rested his head for the night. After only a few hours of well-deserved rest, it began all over again the next morning when he even woke up the roosters with their feed. That's early. I can't imagine such a life of unrelenting drudgery at any age, let alone a boy who took his first breath just ten years earlier. But other aspects of his life deserve added description.

"His payment, $5.00 for six month's work, (three cents a day) was directly funneled to his family back home. His benefits didn't stop there.

"Part of his payment for these back-breaking hours included receiving hand-me-down work clothes. In addition, he could attend school—provided it didn't interfere with his assigned chores. Hearing his schedule, we can safely conclude there were few hours left in the day to attend school. How could he even summon sufficient energy to study? Not surprisingly, people who used such never-ending child labor found the completion of farm chores more critical than the worker learning to read or write. With such priorities foisted upon him, it was no surprise my grandfather quit school after the third grade. That decision he regretted all his life but he knew he'd have to be a good learner in areas other than academics. But he was more resigned to his immediate day-to-day survival. He knew no other choice but to keep working as an indentured farm worker. Note I didn't use the term 'unskilled worker' because he learned skills that would later benefit him. He was occasionally allowed home for a brief bit with his family before he was called on again to serve his role in a way-too-early introduction to family support.

"At fifteen, his servitude on a different farm called for him to wheel sawdust in a wheelbarrow for hours on end. Although lacking formal education, he was smart enough to know he was on a dead end street. Unless he changed his course, he was destined to more of the same. There was no progress, or even hope for progress, down that road. Change was needed.

"He decided to act. At about sixteen, he left that last job and considered options beyond Nova Scotia. Jim had heard stories from other Nova Scotia natives who left to work "up" in Boston. They returned with claims of endless opportunities. They said in America, if someone wants to work, they would be paid handsomely for their efforts. He surely thought *'It has to pay better than the three cents a day I was being paid in my first job.'* Jim Schofield decided to seek his fortunes in what they called the "Boston States."

"He decided to leave his beloved homeland of Nova Scotia, but it had to be kept a secret. That decision would bring anguish to his family, especially his parents. Maybe they harbored guilt with his childhood cut short because of those indentured years. They were certainly worried for his well-being out working those farms but on the farm they at least knew his whereabouts and what he was doing each day. He couldn't just leave them with no word where he went, what he was doing, or what had become of him. Jim needed a confidante and found one in his older sister, Lena. Only she would know his plans. She agreed to keep his leaving a secret providing he sent a letter, as soon as possible, indicating where he was living. He agreed to her terms.

"Lena gave Jim a small Bible provided he send her notification with a return address so she could not only reply but also tell their parents that, although he lived far away, he had signaled his safety.

"Jim, along with a Norwegian buddy, left on a boat for Boston. They arrived in the big city with ten cents between them. Knowing work would be very competitive with others, they made a decision. With that final dime, they invested in a street car ride to the end of the line which included a transfer to a horse car which deposited them in a town called

Milton. Unless they found work there, the term "end of the line" might bring an even more literal meaning.

'At their end of the line, they jumped off the horse car and noticed a nearby depot with large draft horses used to pull wagons. With a sense of familiarity at seeing the animals, formal education or not, he knew his way around horses and approached a man whose body language suggested he was the boss. With a bold look in his eye and an unwavering voice, young Jim confidently asked if there was any work available. The boss, seeing Jim as young, inexperienced, and small in stature, jokingly said, 'Prove you can harness those horses!'

"Evidently, the bossman felt such an order would prove difficult for this newcomer and prepared to watch this kid make a fool of himself. He was wrong, so wrong. Although young and small in stature, Jim was far from inexperienced. It became clear they had misjudged him as they watched him stride into the horse stall with an authoritative air and firmly command the horses to move as directed. The horses responded as ordered as he deftly swung the harnesses on the huge horses. He made it appear to be the easiest thing in the world. Shocked, with his jaw dropped in amazement, the man had no choice but to hire him immediately. Young Jim learned that his background as an indentured worker familiar with farm animals had quickly proven helpful. His experiences six years earlier was an investment in his future. Jim figured it would likely pay much more than the three cents a day he was once paid.

"But he didn't stop there. He knew one job wasn't enough to live on so he networked (as we'd call it now) by asking questions, meeting people, and talking potential employers into giving him a chance to prove himself. Odd jobs started to come his way which included winding the town clock in Milton's Congregational Church. Later, he was hired to light each night and extinguish each morning, the town's gas-powered street lamps. Somehow, he arranged to borrow a horse-drawn wagon for transportation and shared makeshift sleeping quarters in a local horse stable along with his traveling Norwegian buddy from Nova Scotia.

"Following weeks of such work, he remembered his promise to write his sister, Lena. He sat down with pencil and paper with the strongest intention to let her know he had not only landed safely in Boston but found work. Try as he might, he was unable to put the words on paper. Terrified, he admitted to himself he couldn't write the words he wanted. Nothing came out. He wondered to himself '*What has happened to me?*

Why can't I write her in words that I use all the time?' Then the realization hit him.

"He was unable to put pen to paper because he had been out of school a long time and had never really learned how to write. It was out of the question. But all was not lost. At least he could read. He'd figure a way to get it done.

"Being a resourceful soul, he devised a plan to write a note without losing face and asking someone to do it for him. He turned to the Bible (don't we all sooner or later?) for help. With the Holy Bible Lena had given him, along with an almanac he borrowed, he laboriously read searching for the exact word he needed for his sister's letter. He began copying the word he needed from the book as he wrote his letter. Jim figured out a way. He advised his sister that he was doing well and asked her to tell their parents of his whereabouts. That terror of being unable to write plagued him most of his life. Fortunately, he persevered in contacting his parents.

He returned to Nova Scotia, met and married Blanche, and migrated to the United States in 1923 where they raised their children in Massachusetts

---

1891
Coastal Shipping

Once the Civil War ended, America tried to grow in all ways. Their commerce depended on getting goods between points as fast as possible. America's commerce was kept active with the use of clipper ships which not only traveled up and down America's coasts but carried cargo between the east and west coasts. It was a lot quicker to move goods by water rather than over land, especially for goods that were likely to spoil or ruin during transportation.

These schooner and clipper ships were very fast. Schooners were tall and graceful ships having at least two masts. The word "schoon" means to move quickly and smoothly.

These ships hauled most of the same cargo that today's modern trucks haul cross country. Today, however, these same ships are used for pleasure crafts or 'school boats' serving as classrooms.

When I wrote the late Freeman Leonard's life story, "In The Beginning . . . Alpha," I opened with the christening of a schooner named after his mother, Estelle Phinnney. We will learn of its brief and "checkered" travel log.

Estelle Phinney as the nine-year-old daughter of the ship's owner, christened the ship in 1891. Our story begins with that time.

We return to Freeman Leonard's account of the Estelle Phinney:

Estelle Phinney
July 15, 1891 at 10:30 a.m.

East New London, Connecticut

"Carlos Barry gave the signal, 'Let her go!'

"At that point, the hammering of the wedges designed to free the ship began and the sound echoed like many rifles fired at once. The ship slid slowly at first, then gathered momentum as it met the ocean. Just as its bow entered the water, a little girl made a shouted as she brushed the ship's stern with an elegant bouquet of flowers provided by her mother.

"'I christen thee *Estelle Phinney*!'"

"The nine-year-old girl, Estelle Phinney, had just christened a ship named after her. As her namesake entered the water, it floated as graceful as a swan on a lake after a few seconds' settling into its new environment.

"The centerboard schooner *Estelle Phinney* was finished at McDonald and Anderson's Shipyard in East New London, Connecticut in 1891. It was made for Captain James Phinney of Cotuit, MA, who was once employed in a similar position on the schooner *Bill Stowe*. He decided to name the ship after his little daughter who was considered 'accomplished and beautiful.' Incidentally, years later, Captain Phinney had his picture on the cover of the old Buick magazine.

"The *Estelle Phinney*, one of the largest four-masters ever built, was made of the best materials using white oak and chestnut with the highest quality fastenings available. The hold was over 17 feet deep and would carry between 1450 and 1500 tons of cargo. She was 188 feet (well over half a football field in length) with a beam (width) of just over 38 feet.

"She was fitted with steam power for hoisting sails, anchors and pumping. This beautiful schooner was fitted with a wrecking pump capable of pumping water from the hold even if a hole the size of a barrel was opened in her hull.

"The *Estelle Phinney* was to be used for transporting cargo in the "Black Diamond" trade route between Norfolk, Virginia and Boston, Massachusetts. Their "Black Diamond" cargo was usually coal for the Boston and Old Colony railroad. Interestingly, it was built to go through the Old Colony Bridge, which was very narrow.

Rosalie Powell, in her untitled life story, spoke of her paternal grandfather.

1899
My Paternal Grandfather

"I never met my paternal grandfather, William David Humphrey. But I do know he caused considerable news at the turn of the century in Wagoner, Oklahoma, still then an Indian territory. That makes historical sense as the state's name, 'Oklahoma' is a combination of 'okla' meaning 'red' and 'homa' meaning 'man.'

"My Grandfather Humphreys was a Wagoner lawman, either a marshall or sheriff. In the chronicles of crime, lawmen, while fulfilling their duties, have always made enemies. As it turned out, my grandfather had at least one such adversary. At some point in his career, he helped send a convicted man to jail.

"During the sentencing, and throughout his incarceration, that man swore revenge on all responsible for his sentence. Years later, either the man escaped, or served his time, and fulfilled his promise to hunt down all those responsible for his served jail time. Early in 1902, this ex-con caught up with my grandfather and murdered him. My father, son of this murdered lawman, was born Oct. 1, 1899, making him barely two years old at the time."

Chapter 3

The 1900s

December 5, 1906
The *Estelle Phinney* is in Trouble

Wednesday, Dec. 5, 1906

"The *Estelle Phinney* successfully ran the coal and lumber trading business for the next fifteen years between Norfolk and Boston. But trouble visited on Wednesday, Dec. 5, 1906. While en route from Boston to Newport News, the schooner began leaking badly. Fortunately, two ships were nearby and willing to help. The steam pilot boat *Philadelphia* and the tug *Mary Walker* pulled the *Estelle Phinney* ashore at Indian River, three miles south of Rehoboth, Delaware. The ship was in bad condition. On the ocean's edge, she was being pulled by the *Philadelphia* and the *Mary Walker* until they got the ship's stern slightly off shore.

"These ships remained with the schooner until 4 a. m., when the tide would be the highest, Following repairs, they'd try to re-float her. Meanwhile, the wrecking steamer *North America* was on her way from Philadelphia to assist. The *Estelle Phinney* had a full load of lumber which would make the re-floating process more difficult. The operation proved a success as the ship continued on to Newport News, Virginia.

December 29, 1906 (three weeks later)
The *Estelle Phinney* is in *More* Trouble

Saturday, December 29, 1906

"Just over three weeks later, the *Elizabeth Palmer* was on her way to Boston amidst a strong northwest wind which made for a heavy sea. It was on the same path as the fully-loaded *Estelle Phinney*. Both were just offshore from the Barnegat lighthouse in New Jersey. The *Elizabeth Palmer*, measuring 300 feet long, with a 48 foot beam and net tonnage of 2446 tons, was almost twice the size of the *Estelle Phinney*.

"The bow of the larger ship caught the heavily laden *Estelle Phinney* on the starboard side and cut a huge hole in its hull. (larger than the barrel-sized hole the pumps were supposedly capable of handling!). Its highly-acclaimed wrecking pump was useless.

"Once the hole was torn through the ship, there was uncontrollable chaos and confusion. The scene was indescribable with total wreckage, at the point of impact, in the middle of the *Estelle Phinney*. This split prevented those on one end of the ship from helping anyone on the opposite end.

"One lifeboat, in the stern, was freed from the ship. Three crew members made their way safely to it only to watch helplessly as their friends struggled for survival on the sinking bow.

"Moses Wright, the ship's engineer from Bangor, Maine, and his 19-year-old wife, Pearl, were in their cabin mere moments before the collision. Recently married, Moses had her on board as a wedding trip. When they came out to see what had happened, they were separated. As Pearl became tangled in the bow's torn rigging, he was swept overboard. He surfaced only to watch helplessly as Pearl slipped into the ocean after the ship made its last quiver before it plunged straight down. Her body was never recovered. Shortly, Moses Wright was plucked from the ocean by those in the lifeboat.

"The sinking of the *Estelle Phinney* took place in just a few minutes. The survivors were taken aboard the lightly damaged *Elizabeth Palmer* which sustained less than $500 in damage and cruised back to Boston with no loss of life.

"Captain Phinney was home at the time of the accident taking care of his very sick wife."

America has always had its share of heroes. The examples they set for us makes it instructive to anyone studying America so they can pay attention to those folks who have made major sacrifices and contributions.

When you live on an island, as I do, one meets a lot of people who have faced danger on the ocean. I wrote the life story of the late Ralph Brown titled

"Truly Blessed." Ralph, a long-time islander, shared with me several stories of local Martha's Vineyard heroes. Being an island with many folks involved in swimming and boating, there is no shortages of opportunities to help others in need. Ralph's hero had a local flavor with just enough quirks to warrant a re-telling of one of his stories. Ralph told it well.

1910
"Ready to die, Ready to die!"

"Living on the island is sometimes a dangerous life. People in ships passing by or earning their living in deep water are always at peril. For years, islanders often save these folks' lives and become heroes. One such man was Captain Levi Jackson. He was famous in our town for having a reckless disregard for his own personal safety when it came to saving others' lives. In fact, he had a nickname in town of 'Ready To Die.' It was always pronounced by local inhabitants (and Levi himself) as 'Ri-De-Di-Die.' As a young boy impressed by anyone from the sea, I can remember him often saying that phrase.

"I'm going to relate a story demonstrating how Levi Jackson's nickname was highly appropriate. It happened on Sunday, January 23, 1910. A six-masted schooner named *Mertie B. Crowley* was sailing at night on the East Coast of our country during a major storm. This ship measured 296 feet long which made it just four feet short of a full football field. It had no motor, no propeller, just sails.

"It had a full load of coal it had picked up in VA and was heading to Boston.

Captain Haskell and Mrs. Haskell, along with their crew of thirteen, saw a lighthouse flashing which they thought was on Long Island, New York. They were wrong. In fact, the lighthouse they saw was from the Edgartown Harbor on Martha's Vineyard while they were three miles south off Wasque Point. The storm and its fury combined with the strong tides had thrown them way off course.

"They had run aground in the early morning hours on some dangerous shoals. If one didn't know the area it would be quite easy to do as those shoals measured only three feet underwater at certain spots. The ship, stuck on a shoal, was helpless to maneuver and the tremendous waves had broken the ship in two. Captain Haskell had lashed his wife up high on the fore and main masts and later lashed himself as well. The crewmen had done the same to themselves. What a sight it must have been! It was their only hope of staying alive.

"At daybreak, some Edgartown citizens who lived near the beach saw the ship foundering along with the bodies tied to the two masts. They contacted the Woods Hole Coast Guard who left immediately for a rescue attempt. During their passage across the Vineyard Sound the local townspeople went straight to the home of Captain Levi Jackson. If anyone could save these people it would be 'Ri-De-Di-Die' in his 32 ft. fishing sloop, the *Priscilla*. At about 9 a.m. he and a small crew quickly gathered their gear and left from the harbor toward Cape Pogue in one of the roughest seas in memory. It took them almost an hour to reach the foundering ship and by that time the ship had finally split in two leaving only the forward portion (bow) with a few masts and rigging still somewhat above the raging Atlantic.

"They approached the ship very carefully as the storm was not only creating massive waves but the shoals were everywhere, still capable of grounding Captain Jackson. He expertly maneuvered his sloop twice within two hundred yards of the *Mertie B. Crowley* only to have waves drive him back. On his third attempt, he got close enough to throw out his anchor and instruct his men to row out in small fishing dories toward the ship with instructions for the nearly-dead survivors to jump from the rigging into the small dories. This was no easy feat as the timing had to be perfect. The people on the ship alternated being either fifty feet high or level with the dories based on the height of the crashing wave at any given moment.

"The unwritten rule 'Women first!' was applied and this event was no exception. It was hardly an honor, however, to be the first woman (or man for that matter!) to make that leap to a small dory below but the Captain's wife did so successfully. Her timing had to be perfect to catch the boat at it closest considering the pitching sea. Likely through pain, or fear, she fainted in the dory's floor in ice-cold water. The small dories could only carry one person at a time so they had to row back to the *Priscilla*, drop off the rescued person, and row back to get the next. There were three dories rowing back and forth at the same time. Moments after the last of the eleven lashed jumpers was saved, the ship sunk.

"Captain Jackson's problems were not over as he had to safely return to Edgartown with a weighted-down boat while coping with a powerful 'following' sea, generally the most dangerous. The Coast Guard, meanwhile, stayed off at a distance observing the rescue.

"The whole town watched the distant life-saving mission and had a rousing welcome for them when they returned to Edgartown Harbor. The rescue began at 9 A. M. and finished at 4 P. M. It was said to be one of the biggest celebrations in years. The townspeople had established a building on the waterfront with cots and blankets. Many of the women had gallons of steaming coffee brewing over a red-hot stove.

"Captain Levi 'Ri-De-Di-Die' Jackson took it all in stride. One of his favorite lines was "Think nothing of it" whenever he did anything of that nature. He said it and hustled home to see his wife and newly-born son. Later Captain Jackson and each crew member were awarded Carnegie medals for heroism at sea.

"He was a prime example of the dynamic and fascinating people who made old Edgartown what it was."

To begin the Schofields' military thread, my paternal grandmother's Blanche's brother, Dave, deserves mention. This is from my autobiography, "Hey, Jay! What's The Story?"

1916
World War I

"Before the war, in the early 1900s, David Schofield had set up a blacksmith shop. When the war broke out, he enlisted in the Nova Scotia Highlanders, a reserve infantry regiment of the Canadian Forces. He received neither specialized basic training nor combat readiness preparation. On the other hand, his blacksmithing skills were needed at the front line to repair equipment used against the Germans.

"Dave's blacksmithing tent at the front line was located on the famous Hindenburg Line, a large system of defenses in Northeastern France. These fortifications had been constructed by the German, using Russian POWs as labor, during the winter of 1916-17. The defense system had many concrete bunkers and machine gun emplacements, seemingly endless belts of barbed wire, and tunnels for moving troops.

"One day, a German enemy soldier burst out of nowhere into Dave's repair tent and aimed his rifle just inches from Dave's chest. Our Schofield ancestor, with his amazing strength, somehow disarmed the enemy soldier and grabbed him around the throat with one of his powerful hands. With that strong blacksmithing hand, long accustomed to bending steel and gripping hammers, he squeezed tighter and tighter. He watched the soldier's panicked look as he must have felt his life's color draining from his face. Within seconds, Uncle Dave had crushed his windpipe suffocating the enemy. With that interruption set aside, and the body removed, he continued his work repairing equipment."

Dianna Gantt, shares with us a story about an ancestor from her tentatively titled book "Life Gantt Be This Good" taken from the Prohibition days in America:

1920
North Carolina

"Grandpaw Pharr was deeply involved in the North Carolina moonshine industry during the Prohibition era. Moonshining remained a major crime which our government found hard to control. My grandfather had a broad range of talents but the moonshiner folks mostly appreciated his welding skills. He welded the stills' aging seams which often split causing leaks. Grandpaw Pharr left the farm for hours at a time as his welding skills were in great demand. As always, the local economy determines the skills workers develop. The constant maintenance of stills was critical.

"During those days, the feds had a program to somewhat accommodate the moonshiners. There was a period they could make the liquor in their stills and sell it back to the government for resale purposes while they provided a sticker which was attached to each bottle. These stickers were more like federal stamps, or sales tax stickers, like they use today. Although the moonshiners preferred to sell the homemade alcohol to the public, our government wanted it sold only to *them* for tax purposes. Many of them had bottles with no stickers but once the word got out that the revenuers were in town they raced back out to the stills to ensure each bottle had a sticker making it somewhat 'legal' in case a surprise raid took place. They didn't sell it all to the government preferring to sell whatever they could back to their own customers, their friends, probably for a better price. The Prohibition era, so often depicted in today's movies or television shows, means more to me now as I can relate to its events when they are shown on the screen.

———————

Most of us have no idea what it is like to finally arrive in America by way of Ellis Island. Newcomers had heard about it, dreamed about it, and eager to step foot on the island. That first step was surely accompanied by discomfort, anxiety, a possible refusal of entry, and harassment. The doctors there examined these immigrants closely for illness while others judged these people's ability to care for themselves in a strange, new land.

The late Mr. Emanuel Athanas, an immigrant from Greece, shared his story with me when I wrote his memoirs some years ago. His book, titled "Teacher, Journalist, Patriot: The Life Of Emaneul S. Athanas," is loaded with interesting stories Below, he tells his of one such story when he arrived from Greece.

1926
Greece To NYC

"I cannot forget it! Will never forget it! After an 18-day journey aboard the *S.S. Byron* from Pireaus, Greece, I arrived at Ellis Island on August 12, 1926.

"As I waited on the island, I shared the primary worry of the others, the fear of failing any part of the physical examination. It was well known, even among us immigrants, that the American doctors were looking for evidence of trachoma, TB, glaucoma, syphilis, and other contagious diseases. We immigrants were apprehensive; yet, except for concern about my eyes, I remained confident.

"We were in a big room with many benches just sitting and waiting for the dreaded exams. It was like the game 'Follow the Leader.' Thousands of poor immigrants dreamed of a new life, yet one in five were forced back to their homeland if they could not pass either the physical or mental exams. The inspectors asked us many questions. A wrong answer could send you back home. Some of the questions, after giving your name, age, marital status, and occupation would be as follows:

1. What is your nationality?
2. What is your final destination in the United States?

3. Do you have a ticket to your final destination?
4. Do you have money with you? More than $30? How much? Less? How much?
5. Are you going to join a relative? What relative? Name and address?
6. Have you ever been in prison, in a poorhouse, or supported by charity?
7. Are you a polygamist?
8. Are you under contract, expressed or implied, to perform labor in the United States?
9. What is the condition of your health, mental and physical?

"Each morning names were read of those going on to America and those being sent back to their countries.

"Many were detained for the slightest of reasons. If women were without escorts or likely to be public charges, they were held for weeks, and sometimes months. The steamship companies paid the detention expenses and return passage fares for those who were turned away.

"Detainees with medical problems were marked with chalk letters on their clothing: 'E' for eyes, 'L' for lameness, and 'X' for mental disabilities. When people were detained it was agonizing to see the beautiful New York City skyline and the Statue of Liberty, yet be trapped on Ellis Island. Many people were stuck between their home left behind and an unknown life in front. Ellis Island was both a place of potentially great happiness as well as a place of great sorrow.

"Parents were often separated from their children overnight and were forced to sleep in separate rooms. This segregation was based on sex, not age. In addition, we felt like prisoners as the guards herded us from one place to another as we were examined by several doctors and interrogated through interpreters. I went through all the examinations and waited for the results. In frustration I bravely asked a middle-aged woman, one of the Greek interpreters, a question,

"Why do we have to go through all this?"

"She replied rather sternly to me in Greek, 'Krata to stoma sou klisto.' (Keep your mouth shut!)

"Then she smiled and added assurance, 'Ise' en taxi.' (You are O.K. You passed all the examinations!)

"I wanted to embrace and kiss her, but she quickly pointed to the guard. The first step of many had been taken.

"I had spent only one night on Ellis Island. I'll never forget my first American meals: a mushy oatmeal breakfast, a hot dog lunch, and corned beef for supper. I could not finish the last meal. The bread, cabbage, and the potatoes had filled me up. I enjoyed the meals wholeheartedly after the meals served aboard the ship.

Freeman Leonard from his story, "In The Beginning . . . Alpha" following high school, was determined to see the world and joined the military. He had many interesting experiences while seeing different parts of the world. He relates the following story as it unfolds in the jungles of Panama . . .

1928
One At A Time, Please

"I went to a nearby cemetery where native children served as my guides. Surrounding the cemetery was an ancient coral fence which was overgrown with local vegetation. What I saw simply amazed me and the story behind it was even more shocking.

"Near the back of the cemetery were many skeletons piled up with many loose skulls scattered randomly nearby. I asked the kids about one of the skeletons which had been recently placed on the pile and they explained the local custom.

"It seems that each family was provided just one grave. When a family member died, like our culture, he, or she, was placed in the box and buried. That corpse remained in the box until the next family member died. Then, the first box was dug up, its corpse was removed, the second body replaced the first in the box which was then buried again. The first skeleton was moved to the pile in the back of the cemetery. If one family member was buried on a Monday and a second member died on Tuesday; the Monday corpse was removed and placed outside in the back. The Tuesday corpse replaced him, or her, in the box. It seems like an odd process to me but seemed both quite natural and practical to them. I'll never forget the many bones all piled up in the back of the lot.

Eugenia Seamans, in life "Light & Love," provided us with several different perspectives during her story. One describes her family's method for accurate and early determination of the 1928 presidential election results. She explains . . .

1928
Early Knowledge

"In 1928, as a six-year-old, I remember looking up in the sky to see who was being elected to be our country's new president. In that era, few people owned radios which could bring any late-breaking news. Candidate Al Smith was running a supposedly tight race against Herbert Hoover.

"Our only way to determine how the votes were going was to look for an airplane flying overhead. The pilot had pre-arranged signals for us on the ground. If the plane flashed its green lights; it meant that Al Smith was ahead. If it flashed white lights; that told us President Hoover was leading. Many white lights later, Hoover won by a landslide and we were among the first in the country to know."

1929
Playing for Charles Lindbergh

The following segment was from interviews with the late Jim Polk. He chose to only do the interviews with no book. His story concerns Charles Lindbergh as do the next two presentations. The viewpoints from each of my memoirs' clients vary broadly and it is unlikely these three stories of him will ever be told again.

Mr. Polks explains his story as a sixteen-year-old.

"Oh, yeah, the public school system in the city of Boston. I played in the band and Fortunato Sordillo took a liking to me and I guess that I was a fairly competent trumpet player. He ultimately appointed me as president of what they called the 'Boston Public Schools' Symphony Band.' It was a composite band made up of maycbe 100 players made up of the best in the city of Boston.

"By this time, my family had invested $150 into my new trumpet. I remember that band had many functions in the city of Boston. One such privilege to be the honored band onstage when Charles Lindbergh returned to Boston after crossing the Atlantic Ocean.

"I was the lead trumpet and I remember the song I played as a solo for him. It was titled, 'The March From Iedah.' It was a great thrill for me do be selected for this honor and I remember it as if it happened yesterday."

———————————

We are going to hear again from Eugenia Seamans in her book "Light & Love" as she describes going to a tea party when five and meeting Charles Lindbergh . . .

1929
Meeting Charles Lindbergh

"My godfather, Jerry Land, became very important to me and served an ongoing role in my life. He was close with his cousin, Charles Lindbergh, the famous aviator, whose mother was a Land.

"In 1929, after Mr. Lindbergh had flown across the Atlantic, our government ordered him to Washington for conferences. During that visit, he stayed with the Land family in their hotel apartment. Mr. Lindbergh was practically attacked by everybody when he went out on the street because of his immense worldwide popularity. This fame eventually led to his disguise featuring a big hat and false beard. During his two or three weeks' Washington stay, he seldom went out in public. My Aunt Betty Land, Jerry's wife, told Mother that Charles really needed an outing of sorts to see other people rather than his adoring public. Mother offered her solution:

'Why doesn't he come to our house for tea?'

"Aunt Betty agreed it would be a good idea.

"As this little tea party was secret, Mother asked permission to invite some families and their children to meet Mr. Lindbergh.

"As I walked into the room, Jerry, who was always full of fun, introduced me to Mr. Lindbergh, 'This is my goddaughter.'

"Immediately, Mr. Lindbergh sprung into action. He reached down, picked me up by my feet and held me upside-down. I was a long way up as he was 6'4" when I looked into his upside-down face. He soon put this thrilled and important-feeling little girl on her feet.

"He was quite shy and perhaps didn't know what to do with himself. That was, of course, before he met his wife, Mrs. Lindbergh."

For our third connection with Charles Lindbergh we return to Freeman Leonard in his story "In The Beginning . . . Alpha" where he spoke of an American icon, Charles Lindbergh, and his brief connection with him . . .

1929
Watching Charles Lindbergh

"I remember, before I was stationed in Panama, that I saw Charles Lindbergh at Bollin Field in Washington D. C. I wanted to see the famous plane that he had taken on the transatlantic flight in May, 1927. On that day, in D. C., the airport ordered him not to take off on a particular day due to unsuitable conditions. At that field, there was a big cement wall on one end. Not heeding their warning, he decided to leave anyway. I remember some of the airport personnel were hoping he would hit the wall! If I recall, he didn't miss it by much.

"While stationed in Panama, I worked on Charles Lindbergh's famous plane, the *Spirit of St. Louis.* It was ironic that I had seen him only months before at Bollin Field and now again, at Panama. He was preparing for a goodwill flight to Central America and used the Panama field as a stopping-off area for an intermediate check on his plane. I remember him as being stubborn, unkind to others, and seemed kind of 'uppish' to me."

1929
Class Rings

From Freeman Leonard in his story "In the Beginning . . . Alpha," 'A memory came to me about our 1929 high school class rings. Back then, we could buy one for about $2! That's worth mentioning to as a standard of comparison figuring today's rings cost over $200!'

Mr. Emanuel Athanas (Teacher, Journalist, Patriot: The Life of Emanuel Athanas) an immigrant from Greece just five years earlier, had entered college in Worcester. It was a struggle for him as he was both learning the language and trying to finance his way through school by working. This story, although comparatively long, shows some Americans at their best. He shared the following story.

1931
Block Island Blunders, Worcester Wonders, American Ways

"During my college summers, I worked wherever work was available. A friend told me there was an exquisite restaurant on Block Island, located off the coast of the state of Rhode Island. (And, yes, Rhode Island was named after my Greek home of The island of Rhodes in Greece. I'd written articles on it. Through my efforts, Rhode Island and Rhodes Island were in sisterhood in 1995.)

"I was told if I could get a job at that Block Island restaurant, I could make a lot of money. It was meant to be, as there was a job opening on this beautiful island populated by rich people. The summer of 1931 offered me great potential for financial gain.

"The restaurant's dining room captain was Greek. How fortunate! I told the head waiter that I was a student working my way through college and needed a job.

He asked the one question I feared, 'Are you a waiter?'

"I'd been observing the other waiters and answered honestly, 'No, I never worked as a waiter and have no experience.'

"I guess he respected my honesty because he offered me the job.

"Okay, you are a Greek student and I will give you a chance. For one week I'll teach you. Then I'll assign you only one special table that should make you good money. There will be, of course, a small salary to go with the expected tips.

"After the week, he assigned me the 'special' table as promised. During my training, I was instructed to carry the serving tray in my left hand. After arriving at the table, I was to place it on a portable stand before serving the diners.

"Stupidly, with that first special table of customers, I carried the tray in my *right* hand. As I approached the table, I lost control of the tray and dumped it on the party! The soup fell from my tray and spilled all over a young lady. All patrons at the surrounding tables were visibly upset as

I had attracted a lot of attention. The young lady's dress was a mess. She cried out, 'Look what you did to my dress! Look! Look!'

"The Greek captain rushed over and ordered firmly so all could hear, 'Get out of here! Go to the cashier, get paid, and get out of here!'

"I could understand his being upset as he was being judged and responsible for me. Feeling very embarrassed, I left immediately. The young lady, of about nineteen or twenty years, sat there upset with her beautiful dress a soup-stained mess.

"After reporting to the cashier, I got paid and was dismissed. There was no place to go except back to the mainland. I settled on a bench near the ferry as I awaited the ferry to return me to the mainland. It was time to think about getting another job.

As I was sitting there, the young lady whose beautiful dress I had ruined, now wearing a blue jacket and white skirt, was taking an after-dinner walk with her parents. I could see them walking toward me and I pretended to read a newspaper. She approached and sternly identified me as the bumbling waiter, "You are the one!"

"I quickly answered in my most humble tone, 'Yes, I'm sorry! Please send the dress to the cleaner and I'll gladly pay for it.'

"Her mother attempted to restrain her but her daughter became even more assertive while demanding in a firm tone, 'Give me your name and address!'

"At the time, I had no address and told her so. I informed her I was a poor student working my way through Worcester Polytechnic Institute in Worcester, Massachusetts. Hoping to make things better, I told her my name, my Greek name, and wrote it for her along with my college's name and address. I was relieved when they walked away.

"Fresh from being fired, my search for work brought me back to the mainland where I worked as a counterman in a friend's restaurant. The young woman never sent a bill nor did she have any contact with me. I didn't know her name or address so I could not reach her either. As the summer went on I forgot about the incident and was excited about my senior year at Worcester Polytechnic.

1930
My Senior Year

"In September, I returned to the registrar's office, as usual, with my $25 tuition down payment. As always, I was warmly welcomed by Mrs.

Rugg, the director of registration fees. She knew from previous semesters that my visits to her office meant partial payment of the tuition and that the rest would be paid on a monthly basis. Mrs. Rugg never complained if my payment was late. She would always remind me with a sincere smile about my credit status. 'Your credit is very good.'

"This time, however, she would not accept any money and told me so with a smile, obviously very happy for me. She gave me unexpected, but pleasant, news, 'Mr. Ahanas, your tuition is paid in full.'

"I insisted there was a serious mistake but she re-assured me the tuition was paid in full. I knew this could not be true as I hadn't yet made a payment. Something was wrong. Shocked, I walked away pleased but with many questions. I remember thinking I could now apply this $25 toward my books.

"When I approached the bookstore, with my money in hand, I was told that my books had already been paid for. Again, how could this be? The same scene was repeated at the athletic office. All fees had been paid!

"Someone found out all the different fees due and paid them in full. Who was my benefactor? I immediately thought of Mr. Pavlow, the restaurant owner in Meridan, Connecticut, who had driven me to Springfield and bought my books. My suspicion was reasonable since he had sent me a Christmas gift of $100 in my sophomore year. Yet, somehow, it didn't figure. My senior year, from September to June, had other stunning events.

"There were ninety-two in my graduating class of 1932. During my college years, I enjoyed my many friends and professors. They helped me a great deal. I was unhappy because I could not make grades as high as I hoped for. During my four years, I earned a "C" average. Regardless, it was time to graduate!

"Graduation was held in June of 1932 in the gym hall. Little did I know that I was soon to be embarrassed when the president of the college was unable to pronounce my last name. This low moment was quickly replaced, however, by a positive one. While handing me my diploma, he explained to the audience that I was one of only a few graduates who'd worked their way through college. I swelled with pride listening to their thundering applause. It more than made up for his awkward pronunciation of my name.

"As I left the auditorium with diploma in hand, I felt a little depressed. Outside, I leaned against a column in the front of the building. I could see all the other graduates embracing their parents, friends, and other relatives. Congratulations were certainly the order of the day for us. But there were none for me. I was alone and just wanted to cry.

"Quietly, someone approached me from the back and gently tapped me on the shoulder. I turned around and saw someone who looked like a policeman. I wondered had I done something wrong? I felt comforted, however, when I realized he was a uniformed chauffeur. He extended his hand and asked in a formal tone: 'Are you Mr. Athanas?'

"He mispronounced my name but it didn't matter. I shook hands, looked him directly in the eye, and replied. 'Yes, I am.'

"He demanded, 'Come with me.'

"I was shocked. Everything was out of context. For a moment, I hesitated to follow him. I knew I'd done nothing wrong and asked him why he wanted me. With the hint of a smile, he half-ordered and half-asked again, 'Please come with me.'

"I went with him and we approached a beautiful limousine with people inside. As the chauffeur opened the door, I recognized the girl that I had dumped the soup on the previous summer! Her parents were also there with her and they were smiling.

"I was scared! Doing the right thing was important to me. With no hesitation, I leaned toward her window and apologized for ruining her dress a year earlier.

"I followed the apology with a question, 'Please, I hope you brought the bill for the cleaning?'

"She responded with a smile and asked that I get in the car. I did so but my brain was filled with so many thoughts.

"As we drove off, we were introduced; I finally learned her name. It was 'Grace MacKenzie' who had just graduated from Smith College with a degree in Arts. She and her parents asked me many questions about my nationality, my future plans, if I planned to get a Master's Degree, or maybe, someday, a PhD. It was mentioned that her father was a well-known executive in a large company.

"The conversation continued and I made the connection. These were the people who had paid my college bills! No event in my life had prepared me for this situation. How was I to handle it? I wasn't sure but I became determined to help others along the way. America had reached out to me in such a big way and I didn't know how to repay it. 'Grateful' doesn't begin to express my thoughts.

"Grace and I had a relationship for a few years as I went off to work in New York City. While she attended a finishing school in Paris, we continued our friendship through letters. Because of my Greek training to be a gentleman, I was always reluctant to really tell her how deeply I cared for her.

"But her letters from France stopped, I had not received one for several months. Assuming I had done something wrong, I reached her parents seeking answers. I got one answer from them saying that Grace had died in Paris!

"Totally shocked, and in deep remorse for not sharing my true feelings to her, I vowed never to withhold inner feelings toward anyone again for the rest of my life."

1929-1940
The Great Depression

It seemed as America was always undergoing some level of catastrophe and following the 1929 Wall Street Crash we entered The Great Depression and continued approximately to just before WW II. Families lost everything including their ability to earn a living along with whatever savings they had accumulated. It wasn't just in our country but also pretty much throughout the world. But as you will soon see, the effects of the Depression were often dependent on the person and where they lived. I sampled many of my memoirs clients' several stories and prevailing attitudes. I will share several.

The first observation was from Eugenia Seamans in her book "Light & Love":

"Well, the lowest moment in America during my lifetime was The Great Depression. We witnessed it each time we drove across America. As a young observant girl, I remember all the barns' paint was peeling because there was no paint. Whole families stood in bread lines for free food. Homeless people slept in subways, parks, and old empty warehouses. Men who once had jobs sold apples on the street. Thankfully, our family, with our father in the military, kept food on the table and paid the bills. We were surely very fortunate."

---

*On the other hand, Freeman Leonard ("In The Beginning . . . Alpha")
had a whole host of different experiences living on Martha's Vineyard as he
explains below.*

1935
Depression

"I feel the best time in my life was during the Depression Years. It was just all so equal as our friends were in the same fix. We shared many good times. Many of these happy events involved all of us as we visited each others' homes to share birthday parties or almost any other excuse for a get-together. We had few luxuries but did have friends who shared our collective ability to live well off the land. Our friendships meant a lot to us and our lack of money was never a factor. We didn't need much but what we all had, we shared with our friends.

"Here's an example: We were at an all-night birthday party for a friend. As daylight approached, everybody felt they should come to the Leonard's house for breakfast. We lived in the camp on the Lagoon right across from the bridge, beside the Lobster Hatchery. Everybody from the party came to our house for breakfast. We all chipped in with different parts of the meal and had a great time. The group of people we were with never needed much entertainment. We supplied our own playing cards or any other fun activity.

"What made friendships work back then? Sharing a lot of meals was a means to maintaining close friendships. Seeing the same people often kept you abreast of each others' lives and created a much closer-knit community than we have today. To be sure, the pace was slower but it provided extra time for friends and activities.

"Another activity that we enjoyed with our friends was playing cards, especially poker and blackjack. We even enjoyed many games of cribbage on my homemade cribbage boards and seldom needed money. None of us had it even *before* the Depression. We just entertained ourselves endlessly and have done the same all our married lives.

"Again, I must say that the Depression, which affected the rest of the country, didn't create a major impact here on the Vineyard. We were so much better off than those on the mainland. Being self-sufficient was especially helpful with the food issue. We were able to get by quite comfortably as we harvested many of our meals from the ocean. It provided for us. Furthermore, once the government started giving out free food during the Depression, many islanders would not accept it. This was especially true of the older people who, with pride, remembered their long history of 'getting by' with what was available. To rely on any form of handout was not acceptable.

Many people found ways to entertain themselves during those difficult years and likely just as many found humor in some of the ordinary events such as going to the movies. Freeman Leonard, among his many jobs, was a projectionist at a local island theater. He opens new doors of humor for us explaining,

The Movies During The Depression

"Looking back now, I see how things have changed. For instance, would you think now of receiving a dinner plate as you bought your movie ticket? Years ago, it was done to stimulate attendance. With a ticket, the customer received a cup, saucer, plate or whatever they were giving out that night. These items were known as 'Depression Glass,' which are now expensive collector's items. People collected them until they had complete sets of the iridescent, amber-colored glassware. There were many happy movie attendees leaving with not only having watched a movie but with a piece of glassware, often difficult to get during Depression times.

"During the movie's showing, the customers were careful not to break them as they held them in their laps. The plates brought some fun times when I worked with Nelson DeBettencourt in the Vineyard Haven theater nights. He found a way to amuse himself with these carefully held plates.

"Nelson loved to cut up the little light chains and carefully separated the little brass balls. He stood on the baloney, and toseds those little brass balls off their plates in their laps. When the BBs hit the plates below; they made an annoying little noise. Although they didn't injure the plates, it was just enough of a distraction to keep the patrons looking around to see what caused the sound. He would come back into the booth just laughing so hard at the people's reactions. Nelson always wondered what people would think if they saw a grown man tossing hundreds of little brass balls off those plates."

The first life story I wrote was for a man named Joe Didato. His book, (First Generation . . . An Immigrant's Son), speaks of his immigrant father working during the Depression in Connecticut.

1938
Depression Times

"My Dad worked mainly at manual labor jobs always hoping that someday, he'd have his own business. His dream came true when he opened a small grocery store called 'The Public Market.' My parents ran it from 1931 until 1936. He was disappointed when the store was forced to go out of business. Money was scarce as the Depression had arrived and he, being generous, carried many people on credit.

"Disappointment, however, didn't mean discouragement for my dad. He went right back to work but this time in a mill run by the Russell Company. He worked as a weaver making military supplies such as gun and ammunition belts along with parachute harnesses."

Although the following story is not strictly American history, it does shed light as background material on the tragic World War II which we'll be soon reading of in detail as told by several of my clients. That war killed so many of the world's citizens including over one million American soldiers either dead or wounded.

This short story is told by Ilse Beckmann, whose story, ("The Tapestry Of My Life"), presented a powerful portrait of life from a little girl's viewpoint who was age only eight years old.

1930
Hitler

"As a child, it is common to see that not all children are alike. The differences, as in any society, were sometimes mentioned by my classmates. For example, some of the children I went to school with were poor. I remember one girl sitting in front of me with lice in her hair. She was often washed with petroleum and always had a certain smell about her.

"We sometimes heard of adults speaking of people who were 'Jewish.' I didn't know of any Jewish students. There may have been some of mixed background but it had no real meaning for me. There was one girl in the girls' middle school whose father was a Jewish lawyer. She was described as being 'half' Jewish.

"It was a mystery why some Jewish people just disappeared. This would have been around 1930 when I was eight years old. You see, at this time, Hitler wanted no enemies such as a group called 'communists' in his Germany.

"One day, as I was coming from school, I saw what seemed to be a pick-up truck surrounded by a barbed wire fence. There were benches in the truck with people sitting on them. Adults explained to us they were 'communists and spies' who had committed illegal activities. Such people were determined to be guilty. There was no way to prove their innocence.

"They vanished. Where? Adults told us these people went to 'prison.' That seemed only right. After all, adults designated them as 'bad people.' They *should* go to prison.

"We were told there were so many criminals that the prisons couldn't house them all. These spies had to be sent to 'camps.' It was just a matter of available space; that's what we were told. The camps' real purpose, and location, were kept a secret. It was simple: spies were to be punished.

"Years later, after the war ended, we learned that 'prison' in this case, meant 'concentration camp. There is a big difference between those two concepts. Hitler didn't want citizens to know the truth so he could go through with his political plans. Most German people were lied to repeatedly. Keep in mind our only method of communication was the newspapers and radio, both of which were controlled by Hitler's administration.

"In 1933, when I was eleven, our country forced President Hindenburg into appointing Adolph Hitler as chancellor of Germany. Hindenburg always referred to Hitler as 'that Bavarian corporal' who would turn Germany into a dictatorship. Unemployment was up to six million by then and Hitler's Nazis had fought the Communists in many street battles.

"There was uproar in the cities and many shootings. There was no hope. Hitler was viewed as a savior at first even though he was considered a fanatic. The military industrialists of Germany, recognizing he was a fanatic, were convinced they could 'tame' him and his men in brown uniforms with swastika arm bands.

"Hitler had good programs at first and was viewed in a positive light. There were houses for most people and many promises. His ideas even went as far as planning for transportation, namely the Volkswagen. It was considered a car for the people and would be affordable for all.

"The power he'd acquired went to his head. He figured he could conquer the world. It was thought that what *was good for Germany would be good for everyone.* He got bigger and bigger. For working people, he was viewed as a blessing so the many audiences who heard him speak were eager to stab the air with their 'Heil Hitler!' and Seig Heil! salutes. He was not what he was purported to be and hardly a savior for Germany. But as a little girl, I didn't know any better; that would change as I grew older. We were misled by so many people in government."

1930
Gettin' It Done

During the post WW I years, in the mid-1920s, America was in yet another rebuilding stage as many were out of work and the Great Depression had struck. This next offering is from my own life story ("Hey Jay! What's The Story?") I talk about efforts Americans, such as my grandmother's in this story, put forth in trying to help others in time of need as well as helping themselves through rough times. Americans were simply "gettin' it done." Even back then, folks were into the "win-win" concept. Let me explain . . .

"My grandmother, Blanche Schofield, along with raising five children, used her many skills to help put food on the table for her family. She was a talented cook capable of feeding quality meals to many people at one time.

"During the days of the Depression in the 1930s there were some road projects going on near the Schofield home on Ash St. in Weston, MA. Part of the job included the installation of underground water pipes. Men were hired to dig ditches in the area and the Schofield family went to work providing food and drink for these laborers.

"My grandmother would often cook them three meals a day for about twenty-five cents a meal. They would get thirsty and her son, twelve-year-old Brent, would continuously get them water from a nearby stream. He'd fill up the buckets, one after the other, and walk up and down the pipe lines with a dipper giving them drinks.

Son Jay (my father who was eleven at the time) washed the dishes after each of the meals. Dozens of men were fed by the cooperative effort of the Schofields.

"On weekends, the whole family would drive into Haymarket Square in Boston to buy the food necessary to feed the workers the following week. Jim, knowing prices would drop as the night wore on, delayed buying the food until around 10 p.m. to get the most favorable prices. My grandmother, once back in their Weston home, stored the food in the two little iceboxes they had recently bought. It is estimated my father's family continued that effort from 1927 to 1930."

We'll return to Ilse Beckmann for another story on WW II ("The Tapestry of My Life").

1930s
Guenther's father

"Before the war, my father-in-law, who was a teacher, had lost his job because he wouldn't join the Nazi Party.

"The Gestapo would often rudely barge into their house looking for any proof of his lack of loyalty to Germany. They would closely examine all their food using large knives to puncture the containers and help themselves while looking for any evidence to justify jailing him. They found nothing but the whole scene was so intimidating.

"My husband told me that his father would listen to radio nights in order to listen to the BBC . . . the British Broadcasting Company. It was the only source of accurate news. If the Nazis ever found a radio in your house it would be reason for major punishment as they were forbidden.

"My future mother-in-law, her daughter, and my future husband had to sneak around outside the house at night while he was listening to the radio. Their job was to make sure no one outside the house could hear the radio on. It was sad. You couldn't trust anyone as most neighbors or friends would turn you in to the Nazis in order to direct any accusations away from themselves."

Germany's School System
1930s

"School in Germany was much different than here in America. School sessions begin the first day after Easter vacation . . . not in the fall. We would have a summer vacation of about six weeks and then a fall vacation which was 'potato time.' Some of the children had to help harvest the potatoes so a vacation break was scheduled in that time. We would have a Christmas break similar to the one here in America and we'd return to school around the first of the year. School would then continue until a few days before Easter. After Easter we would be in a new grade.

"There were separate buildings for boys and girls. Our teachers were limited to instructing either boys or girls, but never both.

"Germany provided the concept of 'kindergarten' as the word itself means 'a garden of children.' It was not connected with the nearby grade school of older children. Kindergarten was taught on a private basis . . . not by the state. A kindergarten teacher in Germany would be comparable to an American preschool teacher.

"We went to primary school for eight years but after four years there we had to decide what direction we wanted to go for future careers. The choices were a vocational tract or further academic curriculum to prepare for the 'mittelschule' or the 'Gymnasium.'

"The Gymnasium is devoted to the study of high academic learning including languages and is a prerequisite for university studies and professional careers.

"During my school years this setting was the first opportunity for see boys and girls to be in class together.

1935
My Dad's Loss

Larry Dillard, whose story I wrote titled ("Memories From The Life Of Larry Dillard"), grew up in the town of Lindsay, Oklahoma. This story, although short, touches on an American hero and Larry's connection with him.

"The world famous pilot, Wiley Post, was from Maysville, about ten miles from Lindsay. Earlier, he had set the world record by flying around the globe in just over eight days. As boys, Dad and Wiley Post were pretty good friends who often hunted and fished together.

"Tragedy struck on August 15, 1935, when Wiley and humorist Will Rogers were killed in an Alaskan plane crash. At eight, I remember Dad came home from his work as a part-time deputy game ranger and told Mother Wiley had been killed. I can still hear her gasp. He shared what details he knew and was visibly torn up about his friend's death.

———————————

American radio came into popular use in 1921 and it wasn't until 1938 before a radio became a household item in Oklahoma. Oklahoma was the state of our next contributor named Larry Dillard. When I wrote his story, ("Memories From The Life Of Larry Dillard"), I was fascinated with his love of radio when he was a kid. Below, he shares two stories based on his radio experiences.

1938
The Earth Changes

"Our family radio was often the focal point of our evenings. I can recall listening to two of my favorite westerns, *'The Lone Ranger'* and *'Tom Mix.'* My parents and other adults enjoyed a different brand of radio with *"The Lucky Strikes Cigarettes Hit Parade."* In that show, there had been a survey of the previous week's sales of music which resulted in the top ten best songs of the week. They were then played with a live orchestra and different singers.

Earlier, I mentioned my friend, Joe Nelson. On October 30, 1938, when I was eleven, his parents were out of town for the Halloween weekend. It was agreed that Joe would stay with the Dillards. Halloween was on Sunday night. Following Halloween activities, we were waiting to drive Joe back to his parents' house to take care of the livestock. Our living room radio was on. Although we were poor, we did manage to have a Philco radio both in our home and our car. We had turned it on just a little before 8 p. m. and were listening to a radio show out of New York City aired by CBS.

"It was a one hour show titled *'War of the Worlds.'* Oddly enough, it was introduced as an incredible story intended to entertain six million listeners in America on Halloween Night.

"The show started with dance music but was interrupted by a bulletin. It was reported that there were gas explosions taking place on

Mars at that moment. We considered that interesting but the show soon returned to the dance music. Shortly, more bulletins came on which described a flaming object, 90 feet in diameter, had fallen to the ground just outside Trenton, New Jersey.

"It further told of: 'a humming sound' . . . 'something wriggling out' . . . 'large as a bear and glistening like wet leather' . . . 'with a V-shaped mouth having saliva dripping from rimless lips that seemed to quiver and pulsate.'

"Then things got worse as we got in the car to drive Joe home and continued listening to the car's radio. I remember my dad, as he looked to the sky, and wondered,

"Which of those stars is Mars?'

"The radio told of 'poisonous black smoke . . . death rays . . . army was wiped out . . . people dropping like flies . . . people lying dead in the streets . . . the Martians were themselves dying as they had picked up some disease germs.'

"There were four separate announcements during the show that it was purely fiction but that didn't stop people spreading a wave of panic throughout America. Rumors spread even faster among those people who didn't have radios.

"At the end of the show, as we pulled in to Joe's driveway, the announcer came on in his real voice saying:

"' . . . and if your doorbell rings and nobody's there, it was no Martian . . . it's Halloween!'

"Thankfully, we got Joe back home and all was well in Buckeye. But the next 24 hours were really something! The newspapers had many stories about people's reactions to the show:

"A man from Dayton, Ohio, called the newspaper to ask,

"'What time will it be the end of the world?'

"Hundreds of New Yorkers rushed out of their doors with handkerchiefs over their mouths to guard against the Martian gas. People committed suicide throughout America.

"Radio usually provided our evening's fun. It was common for us to *stare* at the radio as it broadcast its shows. We looked at the radio just as today's kids look at television. There was nothing to see but that didn't stop us from watching the radio. Our imaginations had a chance to grow as we could paint our appropriate and creative scenes to match the show's progress. It was good for us, probably more instructional than today's television.

'*The Shadow*' was also a popular radio show. Orson Welles, the voice of '*The Shadow*,' was the same man who narrated the earlier-mentioned '*War of the Worlds*.' Perhaps that's why it seemed so realistic.

"On Sunday nights, Union 76 Oil Company sponsored a show named '*Point Sublime*.' Each story featured a strong moral character-building value. Speaking of radio shows, '*Lum and Abner*' along with '*Amos and Andy*' were other favorites.

"Saturday nights were usually spent winding down from the week by visiting with friends or neighbors. Some of my parents' friends included Orland and Jean Johnson.

"One such Saturday night, my parents drove to the Johnson's' house to pick up Jean and their son, Jimmy, for a ride into town. I didn't want to go with them but my dad insisted. Listening to the scary show "Inner Sanctum" would have been a better choice for a Saturday night. I was still moaning about it when we stopped at the Johnson's. My dad listened to my griping long enough and suggested I get out, listen to the show at their house, and walk home later. I loved the offer.

"I walked into their home, turned up the radio, and settled on the studio couch. When the show came on, I began my 'radio stare.' It opened with the eerie organ music, the squeaky door and the voice:

"Good evening . . . welcome to . . ."

"Just then, the couch began to move an inch or so! Was my imagination in high gear already? It moved again, this time it moved a foot, or more, away from the wall. The movement was real but the voice continued the show's introduction with apparently no concern for my fear:

'. . . *the Inner Sanctum!*'

"I was sitting up straight and scared stiff. The voice returned with its spooky laugh and the couch moved again; this time back to the wall. By then, I was on my feet and headed for the door. I sprinted toward town, about five blocks away. I had no goal other than to run away from that house and its scary radio.

"I found my folks and told them what had happened relating it all in short sentences and short breaths. They laughed . . . How could they? They knew what I didn't: the same moment that radio show came on was the exact moment a powerful earthquake shook Buckeye. I don't believe I ever listened to my favorite program alone again."

There were some other early, and unforgettable, moments of American radio history such as the the 1925 inauguration of Calvin Coolidge, the first on live radio. In 1937, just a year before Larry's stories, was the live broadcast of the Hindenburg crash. Just four years later we heard a Honolulu reporter who had phoned a radio station in NYC and broke the story of the Japanese attack on Pearl Harbor as the live bombs were exploding all around him.

As a retired teacher and proud of my career, I must include this story as part of the American educational system as told by Mr. Athanas from his story ("Teacher, Journalist, Patriot: The Life of Emanuel S. Athanas"). Although lengthy by comparison with other stories, it shows teaching at some of its most innovative moments as practiced in America.

1938
The Conscience

"In 1938, I was teaching part time in a New York City parochial school which was under the auspices of the Greek Orthodox Archdiocese. It was important for Greek immigrants to have their America-born Greek children learn of the Greek cultures and traditions. Our Greek School was held in an American elementary school after the regular daily session.

"Each day, the children ran home for a glass of milk and returned at 4 p.m. for a two hour session with me. It was a sound bargain for the parents as they had to pay $1.50 monthly tuition fee while getting a Greek-born college professor to instruct their children. This fee went directly to the local community church.

"I felt that my students had already put in a full day of learning and needed a short break after an hour's lessons. Halfway through my instructional period, at 5 p.m., I allowed them to visit the school's gym where they played for fifteen minutes, then returned to class. They loved it and worked hard after returning to the classroom. It was always understood they could safely leave their personal items in the classroom when they went to the gym. For a long time, there was no problem with this policy. One event changed that.

"On a winter afternoon, the class had left the classroom for their well-earned recess. After the allotted fifteen minute, the class returned. As one of my young girls approached her desk, she burst into tears. I rushed over to see why.

"Between sobs, she was able to explain that her fifty cent coin, which she'd left on her desk, was missing. I assumed it might have fallen on the floor and briefly checked. Not finding it told me one thing, another student had taken it.

"I announced to the class that we needed her coin back. Thinking while speaking is a valuable teacher's skill. I needed a creative plan while still being sensitive to difficult situations. I made one.

"In my firmest tone, I revealed my plan:

'I am going to shut out the lights. When I do, I want whoever took the coin to toss it against a wall. We will ask no questions as to who took it but just want it back right now. If it lands near anyone in the room we are not to assume it was taken by that person. Am I clear?'

"They half-nodded, indicating it was a good plan. I turned out the lights to achieve total darkness as winter's daylight was gone this late in the day. We all waited anxiously for the coin's thud against the wall then its ringing sound as it settled on the floor. There was neither sound. My mind was spinning with further options.

"What was my next step? I thought back to my childhood and my own school days. *How would my teachers have handled the situation? They would have meted out firm discipline!* I saw no other choice.

"Corporal punishment in those days was quite common, and I'd developed quite a reputation for handing it out. In fact, several of my teaching colleagues would threaten any of their misbehaving students with a visit to Mr. Athanas' room. I was considered the ultimate threat.

"Reluctantly, I turned the lights back on and faced the class. With my stern voice I announced my next step saying,

"'I will shut out the lights again, but this time there will be a punishment for each of you if the coin does not appear. You will each get two whacks with the ruler on each palm, and it will continue until we recover the coin.'

"My hand flipped the light switch down a second time as we all again waited for the coin's sounds. My mind raced. *What's my next option? I needed a creative solution . . . good teachers always have them . . . would I?*

"To this day I can remember wishing that coin was in mid-air and expecting to hear its sound ringing on the floor. But, again there was silence in that darkened room. *Was I making an error in tactics? Could the little girl have been mistaken? Was I going to punish innocent children?* No, I had to stick with my plan of action. The coin still did not appear.

"Giving an extra few seconds, I flipped the switch back on. As promised I grabbed my ruler, had the children stand up at their desks, walked to each of them, except for the crime's victim, and gave them painful whacks on their palms. I didn't like doing it, but my credibility was at stake and there were lessons to be learned.

"I called again for honesty and a 'commitment to conscience' as I threatened to continue the ruler punishment if the coin was not returned. Down went the switch for the third, and final, time. Darkness gave me time to be myself and think of an imaginative resolution. As I was running out of time, it hit me! I had a half dollar in my pocket and if I tossed it, the problem could be over. But what would it teach? I had no answer knowing it was a temporary fix, at best. I threw it toward a corner . . . not near the children.

"I heard the children stirring with relief as the lights were turned on. They looked around with big smiles and started clapping their sore hands and shouting with joy.

"'The coin! The coin!'

"I spoke, interrupting their happiness with some closing thoughts saying,

"'I'm glad. I'm glad somebody finally decided to avoid this punishment for the rest of their classmates. Your conscience is a very important part of you as a person.'

"Seemingly, the episode ended on a happy note. The little girl was happy; I was happy, (as I was running out of ideas!) the class was happy knowing their sore palms would soon heal; and the thief was happy figuring their successful crime had been committed. It bothered me that a thief was rewarded for dishonesty. I had no idea how it would end. But, for then, in 1938, it was over.

In her book, ("Life Gantt Be This Great") Dianna Gantt, shares a humorous story about her dad while he was in the Navy.

1939

Philippine Islands

"Following his western adventures, he returned to North Carolina. One of his younger brothers had briefly dated a woman but once that woman met my father, she 'changed brothers.' The two struck up a relationship and romantic sparks flew. My father, sensing a potential wife, had no immediate job so chose to join the U.S. Navy while she remained in Statesville, North Carolina.

"Following basic training, he served his country aboard a ship whose home port was the Philippine Islands. Father, a regular sailor while highly adventuresome, looked around the ship for new jobs. He desperately needed some tailor work done on his uniform which brought him to the ship's tailor shop. During that visit, Father sensed the job was a 'cushy' one which he might enjoy. In his brazen, confident way he applied for the job claiming his 'considerable experience' as a tailor back home would help the navy. His convincing tone must have done the job. My father was put on the staff but under the watchful eye of the head of the ship's tailor shop.

"Somehow, his immediate work never revealed that his hands had never held a sewing needle. Once he got by the early steps safely under the watchful eyes of others, his confidence took over. Surely a quick study, he could learn one skill at a time faking it as he went along. Clearly, he had faked his skills well enough early on to verify his background as a tailor before becoming a sailer.

"Father became quite accomplished in his new trade. For evidence that he could bring home, he had an idea. He wanted to make a coat that would fit his girlfriend back home. How did he get the right measurements? Simple. He studied his fellow sailors until he discovered one who appeared to be the same size as his girl back home.

"After explaining his project to the man, he asked to take his measurements. After doing so, he cut the material, made the coat to those specifications, and brought it back home. By the time his naval tour was over, he had become head of the ship's tailor shop.

"When he returned to Statesville, he gave his girlfriend the custom-made coat he'd tailored. She must have liked it just fine and, sensing they'd make a good fit, agreed to marry him when she turned twenty-one. She, like so many others, must have sensed he had promise. If he continued to make her laugh, she figured it would all be good."

Freeman Leonard, whom we met earlier, worked an array of interesting jobs but one of the most, in my view, was making model ships for a man named Charles Van Ryper. He explains how the business became connected with WW II.

June of 1941
Before Pearl Harbor

"Charles Van Ryper, my boss, was an interesting man. In the early 1930's, while living in Maine, he started making ship models for fun at a camp on the Penobscot River. People really liked them and commissioned him to make models of actual vessels they'd once been on or perhaps owned. They provided photos of liners, freighters and even some private yachts. From them, he created miniature models. A hobby flourished into an unexpected business. He dropped his intended careers in drama and journalism and taught himself the complicated trade of making models. It was to his liking so, in 1933, he moved his business to Martha's Vineyard where there were many old sailing ships. He found the weather-beaten town of Vineyard Haven to be perfect for his needs.

"He created America's most unique shipyard during World War II . . . right here in Vineyard Haven. Shortly after his arrival on the Vineyard, he developed a reputation for quality work. He first specialized in island steamers and transatlantic liners. But a new priority developed.

"One day in the middle of June in 1941, a man dressed in military attire walked in our shop. He looked around to make sure no one else was in the shop at the time and asked Mr. Van Ryper if he could speak with him with no other customers around. My boss consented and the man began,

'As you can see, I work for the government and we are interested in hiring you to help us out. We feel that Japan is not going to be all that friendly to us in the near future and we want to commission you to build a series of model ships, both military and commercial, for teaching American fighter pilots ship identification.

"The U.S. Navy needed his services. This was the summer of '41. Our government felt Japan could be an enemy six months before Pearl Harbor. We were hired to make 2300 built-to-scale miniatures from only limited information with photos furnished by the Navy. And they had to be built yesterday! Wartime strategy needed models of the entire Japanese fighting fleet, all 23 different vessels. Why? American military pilots needed an instant education to correctly identify our potential enemy's ships. In time, the photos arrived and we began making miniature wooden ships for our fighter pilots.

"Thousands of the models we built were sent to aviators across the country to identify silhouettes and deck plans of enemy ships. This identification process had to be done while looking down through lenses that gave different impressions of altitude. The pilots flew at varying heights from ships so their knowledge had to include details from a distance. The plans for the ships were stolen by our spies overseas and later relayed to Mr. Van Ryper by the War Department, (now known as the 'Department of Defense.') It was clear that photographs could never match a model for exactness. They had to all be made from scratch, by hand.

"Our models were so effective in helping American pilots identify ships that the Navy, once we were in a full scale war including Germany, asked even more of us. We were given orders to also make small-scale copies of both German and Italian fighting ships. More enemies meant more vessels. I wasn't an active participant in the combat missions but I felt I contributed to the war effort through those models.

"Our fame grew. But so did demands. We were approached by the United States Maritime Commission to build models of every type of merchant ship built in American shipyards during wartime. They ordered *six* models of every design that came off American drafting boards. To ensure quality, the government sent Naval inspectors to our Vineyard Haven shop to inspect our work before they paid us. No problem. We did good work.

"Months later, a naval officer entered the shop adorned with all kinds of braid, ribbons and awards. His visit was to decide whether or not we should be awarded a certain unknown military contract. I couldn't help but notice his various awards and had to comment:

'For a little shop like this you're wearing an awful lot of stuff.'

"He replied with an air of confidence:

'Young man, I'm second in the country. When you get this job, and you're going to get it, you'll know why I am here.'

"Familiar with our work, he had come with a secret order to turn out a new batch of model boats and bombers, in case the war took a terrible and unexpected turn. They had hired us to make boats and bombers which belonged to the Soviet Union! Talk about being shocked! The

Russians were our allies but our navy still wanted models made of any potential enemy's ships.

An Example

"We even built a submarine that was eight inches long and painted it a natural color. Then we made another one half its length, four inches, and painted it a darker color. Then we made one half-sized again so it was two inches long yet still contained the necessary detail as the original eight-inch model. For that job alone, we had to make twenty models of each. After each sub was made, it was displayed on a track to enhance the view from all directions.

"Even though I was considerable past military age I felt that we were making a difference as the war continued on. We were the only company that made models for America during WW II. Perhaps, we hastened the war's end. I'd like to think we did just that."

I am thrilled that this story has been told. It would unlikely ever be shared if it weren't for Freeman sharing it with me years ago. There is no publicity on the effort expended on Van Ryper's behalf to aid America with a most unusual contribution.

December 7, 1941
Pearl Harbor

Nancy Miller, another memoirs client from Oklahoma, shared with me her life history which she titled ("This Is My Story—My Life.") She learned of Pearl Harbor in a most unique method which she shares below:

"When Pearl Harbor was bombed, I was attending a Washington Redskins home football game with my cousin's husband, Buck Buchanan as his wife was home with her baby. Nothing was said inside the stadium about the tragedy until an announcement over the public address system requested all members of the armed services to report to their respective bases. That report was stated calmly with the military responding and the rest of the fans continuing to watch the game. Then, in about 5-10 minute intervals, other announcements were made, requesting those staff members of the White House, the FBI, the War Dept., the Navy Dept. to please report to their respective departments. Then people in the stadium started commentating, 'something must be happening.' There was never any knowledge of what had happened nor did hysteria or stampeding for the exits occur. This lack of panic was due to the calmness of the announcer who we later read, knew what had happened.

"The minute we left the stadium, the shouts of 'Extra! Extra!' echoed on the streets with headlines of "Japs Bomb Pearl Harbor." The following days at school were sad, but memorable as we witnessed historical moments—the burning of the Japanese papers behind their Embassy, and turmoil on Embassy row. Downtown, the military was everywhere patrolling with machine guns. The next day, again, all schools gave their entire student bodies permission to watch any proceedings at the Capitol, Congress and Senate. We saw President Roosevelt arrive at the Capital rotunda of the Congress to make his speech to declare war on Japan. We also attended the third inauguration parade of President Roosevelt."

December 7, 1941
Pearl Harbor

The following account of the Pearl Harbor attack is from Ginny Davis ("Virginia's Voyages") whose father was a naval officer recently stationed on Hawaii's Oahu and planning to move his family back in Boston to be with him in Hawaii.

"In the fall of '41, just months before Pearl Harbor, our father had been in charge of safety for the freighters crossing between the United States and England. His primary assignment was to attack Germany's U-boats (subs) as they had attacked American ships, within our convoys, which brought supplies to England. Britain's very survival was dependent upon these convoys. He patrolled the North Atlantic for that horribly cold fall and sunk his first submarine which I later found described in his personal papers. All the debris surfaced, just like the movies; it was terrible. A movie describing that Good Shepherd Program was later made. Just before Pearl Harbor, he was transferred to California and remained in "war stance" for a considerable time."

"Everyone seems to be able to link up their lives with this American event. Although I mentioned it earlier, I'd like to cover it in a bit more detail here. We were in Winchester and I was packing for Hawaii. That Saturday night, Dec. 6, 1941, my then boyfriend's parents had taken us to the movies. My mother stayed at home as we children were off doing our thing. As I returned, my sister Ruthie came running in from her girlfriend's house blurting,

'Turn on the radio!'

My mother was cozily sitting by the fire and listening to one of her many records. This unfailingly soothed her when my father was away. Ruthie ran in and told us the Japanese had bombed Pearl Harbor. We ran to the radio, snapped it on, and listened with our mother. My mother was devastated because it was the first we'd heard this shocking news. The report was sketchy but we could put some of the pieces together after looking at a world map.

"In the meantime, my father had sailed on to Hawaii and his ship was moored near Pearl City. On the morning of December 7, 1941 he had boarded the officers' 'gig,' a small, fast, motorboat which came with a driver. My father had gone ashore at 7 a.m. on that fateful morning to secure our family's housing so we could join him in Hawaii as soon as possible.

"My father had just arrived on shore when the Japanese planes began their attack. Seeing the carnage, he decided it would be best to get back to his own ship and take command. He turned around immediately to return to his ship where confusion reigned. The other men near him also needed to get back to their ships so he began to taxi them back.

"Unfortunately, one of those very ships, the *U.S.S. Nevada*, was on Battleship Row with the others lined up at the dock. As they were hitching up to the boat to discharge the officer, the ship was bombed and began sinking fast. The impact of the bomb knocked the men on the gig into the water, including my father who suffered a scalp laceration from flying fragments.

"Just seconds earlier, giant geysers of water shot into the air all around my father as torpedoes, which had been launched from planes and subs alike, were streaming through the water toward the destroyers' hulls. In seconds, those torpedoes had penetrated the hulls of the destroyers which released millions of gallons of fuel onto the water's surface. There was an oily goo several inches thick on top of the water, much of it on fire. My father had no choice. Fully clothed with his new suit and shoes, he dove into the flaming ocean.

For self-preservation, he took a big gulp of air, dropped below the surface, and removed his shoes. He surfaced quickly, took another big breath, got his direction to shore, and dove under the fiery ocean to swim underwater toward land. Like all navy personnel, he had been trained to break the flaming surface when coming up for air. They were taught to push their hands away from each other to momentarily separate the burning oil. Each time he came up for air he had to quickly repeat this process to create a brief air opening so he could get his next gasp of smoky air for his next dive.

"During this struggle for survival, he realized he had received some sort of head injury from the blast but his first priority was to reach shore without getting burned. His bleeding scalp was of secondary importance. Along with the flaming ocean, burning debris and projectiles were exploding all around him. Many men had become coated with oil and were on fire. Aflame, they swam toward Ford Island while diving underwater to douse their flaming clothing. Some made it to shore, others perished. Upon reaching shore, my father was relieved to see a temporary hospital had been set up where he received stitches for his head wound. Shortly after his treatment, he became concerned about his ship, the *Medusa,* and left the hospital early in the afternoon with his head wrapped in bandages. He needed to go to work.

"The *Medusa* had been anchored at Pearl City with two other destroyers. They were tied up along the west side of Ford Island. He arrived to chaos finding his crew frantically doing repairs. On the way back to the *Medusa,* he noticed the *U.S.S. West Virginia* (his former ship when stationed in Australia) had also been hit and was sinking fast. Off its stern, my father found the overturned *U.S.S. Oklahoma.* These two ships were the outboard ships in the center of 'Battleship Row.' They each had their port sides torn open by torpedoes.

"As my father approached the *Oklahoma's* hull he could hear men shouting for help and pounding on its hull from inside. Their breathing was limited to the remaining air which had been trapped in small air pockets.

"My father quickly assembled his crew and they began cutting through the hull with torches. The next afternoon, my mother got a short cable from our father simply saying, *'All's well. I'll be in touch.'* He couldn't call as the phones were all down and jammed. The next day, at school, someone came to the house and gave my mother a letter from the Commander-in Chief which announced my father had been seriously injured during the sneak attack. It stressed he was safe in the hospital and they would monitor his condition. The implied message was we could not even temporarily re-locate to California without securing Hawaii housing first.

"After 72 hours, they broke through the hull to save many of the *Oklahoma* sailors trapped inside who were suffocating and about to run out of air. Sadly, 429 men perished in that overturned ship but my father's efforts certainly reduced that number. Other overturned ships' trapped members were less fortunate as they kept tapping for two weeks while other crews tried in vain to release them. Sadly, their taps signaling hope for their rescue stopped Christmas Eve.

"Needless to say, my father, and his valiant crew, were recognized as heroes immediately by fellow sailors, and later by the U.S. government following a studied review of the day's events."

"Following his recovery, he was assigned to command 17 destroyers, depart Hawaii to the west, and recover the islands Japan had invaded. He went straight north to the Aleutians. His job was to protect the submarines from attack.

———————————

Bob Morgan was another Martha's Vineyard native who shared his story with me which he titled "The Life and Times of Bob Morgan, Storyteller Extraordinaire" He enters our story just as WW II broke out and shared with us his remembrances of Pearl Harbor along with two poems.

December 7, 1941
Pearl Harbor

"At an early age, I knew I wanted to fly. As a senior in high school, I was sure that I was going to the Royal Canadian Air Force in Canada. A friend of mine, John Gillespie Magee, lived on the Vineyard for only a few weeks after he had turned down admission to Yale in order to volunteer for the Royal Canadian Air Force. We said our "Goodbyes" one day and he went to Canada to join the RCAF signing up for flight lessons at 18. Sadly, he was killed in an air battle over England on Dec. 11, 1941. At that young age he was already an accomplished, self-published poet. All he talked about when he was here on the Vineyard was probably not returning to England.

"John wrote the first classic poem of World War II. It was titled 'High Flight.' On one of his test flights, he wrote back to his mother after landing, that he had just written half of a poem while he was flying. He told her he was going to finish it as soon as he returned to the ground. I would like to include the closing lines of that poem here. It was written on the back of a letter to his mother.

High Flight

'Up, up the long delirious burning blue
I've topped the wind-swept heights with easy grace
Where never lark or even eagle flew
And, while with silent lifting mind I've trod
The high untrespassed sanctity of space,
Put out my hand and touched the face of God.'

"I came across this information as it was printed up in *The Boston Globe* and was very moved by it knowing that he was my friend.

"I continued working for my Grandpa Taylor through that early 1941 winter until shortly after the December 7th bombing of Pearl Harbor. I remember that infamous date and how I learned of our national tragedy that Sunday morning:

"Ken Grant, probably my best friend at that time, had a racer built out of a V-8 Ford that someone had built earlier. His father had bought it for Ken. That Sunday morning, Ken and I were going up to Vineyard Haven in that racing car to go to a restaurant where we had earlier met some girls. The restaurant was beside where Renear's Garage used to be. It is now the Cape and Vineyard office. Our plan was to have some coffee and doughnuts which we had done many times before. Once we arrived there, someone in the restaurant explained to us what had happened hours before in Hawaii.

"The first thing we thought of was *Oh my Lord, supposing we have a war?* Most Americans knew such would be our next step. Admittedly, the Pearl Harbor bombing was very remote from us here on the east coast but it was something we thought would develop into something much more serious and have far-reaching effects on all of us.

"As if it were a movie I watched just yesterday, I remember many loud booms we could hear off Edgartown's South Beach. They happened both before and after Pearl Harbor. There were big guns practicing firing from the battleship *North Carolina* positioned quite a ways off shore. Those sounds were just so loud that their sound waves and concussion effect would just shake the Vineyard like an earthquake. The windows in the First National store would rattle to the point that we thought they would shatter.

"Both before and during Pearl Harbor I would say that I, like most young people of that era, were pretty much focused on the goings-on of Edgartown and very little thought was ever extended beyond our island interests. I might add that, because I did love geography and history, I probably understood a bit more than most my age. Thoughts of war were frightening and came as a surprise to us all. It wasn't something we could visualize like today where we can read about Iraq and watch the war live as it develops.

"Just a month after Pearl Harbor, on January of 1942, I was still upset someone would pull such a sneak attack on our country. Along with several of my friends, at eighteen years old, I joined the military.

"There was no doubt that we were in the right as far as getting involved after Japan's sneak attack. There were hundreds of thousands of people like me who signed up as quickly as they could. We were eager to go. No one could harbor any isolationist feelings as we entered war. There was an unusual feature of World War II in that we were fighting two entirely different wars at the same time. We fought in the hot climates against the Japanese to ten feet of snow against the Germans. It was just amazing to me to think that there were people in combat under such difficult conditions. I was fortunate enough not to have been involved directly.

"I believe I took my oath for the Army Air Corps on January 7, exactly one month after Pearl Harbor. That term, 'Army Air Corps,' was the group's name before it got changed to today's 'United States Air Force.' It was a "Command" before it was actually the Air Force as we know it now. The Air Corps was under the auspices of the United States Army until 1947, two years after the war ended.

My Poem

During my military years, I was obviously quite moved by the whole experience and, while stationed on Santa Maria Island in the Azores, it crossed my mind to write a poem outlining just how many of us who flew in the military really felt many times while airborne. The title of my poem was:

To Fly in Fright

Heaving upward where dead men rest
Leaving earth's winged clipped ones behind
Moving nearer to God's finest
Into a world of another kind.
Of men who parted but not in vain
Of men whose hope were not to die
But if I must, in God's domain
Please let Thy winged wanders fly
In a nonchalant and careful way
And, when our lives have passed us by
We will return to You that day.
With so many thanks for Your guidance through
Those days we needed Your protective light
With humble apologies direct to You
For all those times we flew in fright.
Knowing but doubting that You were there
For every second we spanned the sky
Now we know of Your thought to care
Thank You Lord of all on High.

Larry Dillard, our friend from Oklahoma ("Memories From The Life Of Larry Dillard") from whom we heard earlier, shared with us his recollection of the attack on Pearl Harbor and referred to it appropriately as "The Day the World Changed."

December 7, 1941
Pearl Harbor

"I was just fourteen years old on that infamous day.

"Dad, Red Berry and I were fishing on the Verde River near Camp Verde. But, we didn't get to fish much as we had to hide in the car after being chased by some wild cattle. We did nothing to provoke them but my guess is they would have been pretty mean if they had caught us. As we waited in the car, there was no need to turn on the car's radio as we knew its reception was weak in the mountains.

"My mother and Paula had spent that same day in Phoenix watching a 'walkathon,' a popular endurance ordeal done back then. At the end of the day, we were to pick them up but, on the way, decided to stop at a diner for a bite to eat. We heard the man behind the counter mumbling something about those '&%#$ Japs.' My dad couldn't understand just what the man was griping about and asked. The man was shocked we'd heard nothing as we'd not used our radio. After a brief explanation about a sneak attack, the man produced an early edition paper with an 'EXTRA!' in large, bold print. It described a thumbnail sketch of the sneak attack on Pearl Harbor. In shock, we picked up Mom and Paula and spoke of the day's events. Clearly, things were about to be different.

"We returned to school on Monday, the day after, and had an assembly in the auditorium where we listened to President Roosevelt's speech which was broadcast nationwide. It was a somber occasion. Men of all ages were enlisting in the military to fight for our country. In fact, Red Berry, our fishing partner, enlisted in the navy the following day. In just a few days he, like so many other young Americans, were gone. I saw him only one time after that when he came home on leave following boot camp.

"My cousin, Bobby Dillard, had come to Buckeye several months before Pearl Harbor and lived with us for a while as he searched for work. Finding none, he joined the Army and was stationed in Honolulu, Hawaii, when Pearl Harbor was attacked. In fact, on that day, he was on a barge crossing the harbor when the Japanese planes attacked. He jumped right into the action and fought back with a machine gun. Bobby was credited with shooting down the first Japanese plane of the war.

"Later, he was involved in some of the Pacific invasions and shared with us some of the horror stories of the battles he had experienced."

Our newcomer is a man named David Kestenberg whom I met, along with his lovely wife, Sarah, at a chance encounter in a supermarket in the spring of 2008. I had initiated contact after noting he was wearing a Star of David on a white baseball hat. We immediately seemed to "click" into conversation and one thing led to another. Before long, he shared with me that he was an Auschwitz survivor and indicated he was eager for someone to write his life story. What a coincidence! I explained that's what I did citing my biography service, "Memoirs Matter."

Enthusiastic, he asked me to write an "audition piece" based on a DVD he'd done during an interview for the Holocaust Museum. I wrote this somewhat lengthy manuscript based on his own words from the DVD along with considerable research on my part. Although he enjoyed it, we never got a chance to continue with his project as he died a few months later on Thanksgiving Day. Below is that same manuscript I titled "The Book That Never Happened."

I am so thankful to receive his wife Sarah's permission, along with that of his adult children, to share David's gripping heroic story. They are very proud of his contribution to Holocaust history and this small portion of his story can finally be seen in print. I wish you "Shalom" and pray I have done your story justice.

1939
The Jewish From Poland and The Holocaust

"When I consider sharing my life with others I want them to know of my emotional state during those Holocaust years. Of course, the events, dates and places in any historical narrative are important to scholars of history but often omit the subject's emotions. Yet, such feelings form the foundation for total understanding. I want my readers to think as I thought, make the lightning-quick decisions as I had to do, and experience both the silence and horror I lived. Hopefully, they will never have to live it and only have to study it through the printed word. At times, you may find reading this account is a bit like wading through a sewer knowing that humans could treat other humans as we Jews were treated during the war.

"Clearly, there is no shortage of Holocaust history. The real shortage is the remaining people who lived it. Few saw the sights, breathed the fumes, ate the food, or touched the bodies as I did. Such experiences created my character as it is today. The difficult decisions were done so when faced with continuous danger.

"Each day brought two choices: either adjust or perish. Adjusting to unpredictable events allowed me to live out that day. Self-preservation, one of nature's first laws, helped me develop my mantra: 'One Day At A Time.' I did what I had to do and lived to tell it. I now have the opportunity to grant my father's wish by sharing our story.

I Grew Up Fast

"Above is one of the four-word phrases that can best describe my experience as a Holocaust survivor. I *did* grow up fast. That short message works. It works because my life mirrors very few people still alive. Why did the others die? They died because Adolph HItler, who came to power in 1933, decided our Jewish heritage, our talented people, our so-called 'chosen race' were each responsible for Germany's bad times in the post WW I years. Their economic downturn resulted in blaming others, in finding scapegoats. Jews, became Germany's scapegoats and paid dearly. My own 'payment' began In 1942, at age 14, in Lodz, Poland. Yes, I grew up fast, here's why . . .

Lodz

"In 1933, as a five-year-old, I knew little about Hitler's impact. On the other hand, the rest of the world had been watching with deep concern wondering what the coming times would bring. Surely, Jews were being persecuted in other places but other countries hoped it would be contained within Germany's borders.

"But soon, those hopes were dashed. His hatred toward the Jews extended beyond German borders when he attacked, then occupied, other countries. These countries then fell under German rule as dictated by Hitler's agenda to eradicate Jews, take over the world, and establish the Aryan race as superior.

"His attack on our people began in Poland on September 1, 1939, when I was just 11 years old. Regrettably, Poland fell in just three weeks.

"Within a week, German soldiers had reached, then occupied, our city of Lodz. Why did Hitler target Lodz? After Warsaw, it was Poland's second largest Jewish community. His attack on my city made it personal for me. I was just learning to learn and love my Jewish heritage. At the time, I had no idea how difficult my struggle would be.

The Ghetto

"Germans are a very organized and efficient people. Just three months after they took over Lodz, it was decided to contain all Jews in one location: the "ghetto." It was to be my new home. The Jewish elders told me the Nazis wanted us together so that we could either be killed locally or transported elsewhere and killed later. They needed time to formulate their plans reducing time required and increasing their killing efficiency. In addition, they wanted us centrally located so they could steal our treasures which they assumed we had hoarded.

"But, through it all, I continued to be a boy full of questions: *Why had we moved out of our home? Had I done something wrong? Had my family done something wrong? Why couldn't I take my belongings? I remember thinking we all must have done something really bad as our friends were also sent to this ghetto.*

"The answers from my father went something like this:

"'We must move because we are told to by the Germans. No, you did nothing wrong. We as a family, did nothing wrong except we are Jewish. You see, other families had to move yet they did nothing wrong. You couldn't bring what you wanted as we were given only a few minutes to pack.'"

"I felt confused and scared. Like me, 11-year-old boys had no survival skills for Nazis in the neighborhood. But I vowed that would change.

"By early March of 1940, most Jews lived in their new ghetto quarters, such as they were. Our family remained together but we were tightly packed. Each room in the ghetto housed between three and four people. Not only were we restricted to small housing quarters but the ghetto soon became enclosed with a bricked wall built by Jews forced to do so. The bricks came from the buildings the Germans had already destroyed. It all happened so fast. As I was still confused, my father tried to assure me our new place reflected not what we did but rather who we were . . . Jews.

"Until then, I lived a normal life as a student, a son, a brother, and a friend to many. But those roles soon diminished with the loss of my youthful innocence. I became a young Jew on the run in search of food, shelter and security. As the struggle heightened, so did my Jewish pride. I started to connect with my Jewish history of abuse. Jewish history's persecution became visible; it was no longer stories. Despite this, I began to feel a swelling inside bolstering my Jewish faith. But admittedly, many times my faith clashed openly with my fears.

"Life's cruel twist caused me to focus on what would work to survive. My environment had become one of constant horrors: the screaming of innocent people from Nazi abuse, the random beatings, gunshot victims bleeding to death on the side of the road, and the starving, desperate people stealing to stay alive.

"Miracles were needed but I learned that just staying alive another day was miracle enough. There was little hope as Jews were shot daily for no reason. If a Jew even looked the wrong way, were in wrong place at the wrong time, even if they walked too slowly they were killed. I was afraid all the time.

"It was like being a flood victim where one got sucked into the flow of floating debris doing anything possible to escape the swirling water toward eventual drowning. I needed to build the strength to help my family survive.

"Gradually, I began making more decisions once reserved for my father who was failing. Despite my fierce loyalty to him, I began to question some of his ideas. He welcomed my input; my contributions were no longer viewed as those of a young boy. When he began to value my ideas, it triggered a transformation: the beginning of a role reversal as I began the family's caretaker. Keeping our family alive consumed me.

"We 230,000 Jews in Lodz became a major problem for the Nazi occupiers. They chose to hand off their predicament to a Jewish person. A man named Rumkowski was assigned to organize the ghetto. He became famous on September 4, 1942, when he demanded the message below. This four-word message shaped my life:

"Give Me Your Children!"

"For emphasis, let me repeat that these four words have stuck in my mind as the most powerful, unbelievable, and unreal I've ever heard. To gauge the power of these four simple words one has only to imagine what this demand meant to Jewish families. He wanted parents to simply hand over their beloved children to death camps.

"The families were scheduled to go to Chelmno, a killing station established specifically to annihilate Jews. Once there, the Nazis used trucks which were sealed airtight to contain the motor's carbon monoxide fumes. Those same toxic fumes were piped directly into the trucks which killed all passengers in minutes. This practice preceded the more efficient gas chambers used later on a much larger scale.

"The first shipment was for children, old people, and the sick. It was a horrifying situation for the Jews of Europe, and one to be repeated over and over.

"As it turned out, those four words, 'Give Me Your Children' have led to one of the worst experiences for mankind, resulting in over 6 million people killed in an ongoing mass murder. No words can accurately describe this massive crime perpetuated on the Jews.

"How could that deportation for death be even worse than death itself? Death at least had a finishing point which brought peace. The alive were left in a living hell unaware what the next minute would bring. The phrase 'living hell' must have had its origins in the Holocaust. For me, and countless other survivors, it *was* a living hell.

"In retrospect, many Jews, myself included, viewed Rumkowski with mixed emotions. That was part of the Nazi strategy: to pit Jews against Jews in order to crush their spirit. Some feel he helped the Nazis murder fellow Jews while others felt he saved many Jewish lives in Lodz. It may have been a combination of both. I lean more toward believing he was doing what he felt was right for the ghetto's inhabitants. But the Nazis lied to him as he too was later forced into a death camp.

Sadly, as I grew older after the war, I learned more truths. When the Russians overran Warsaw, the Germans ran away. But the Polish Army, the anti-Semite underground fighters, were against us. They fought and killed the Jews as they wouldn't let them join forces with either the Russians or the partisans. People ran into the forests for freedom which extended over fifty miles.

Trapped

"We lived day-to-day in the ghetto between 1940 and 1942. Survival was contingent upon getting enough food. There were 230,000 of us in a confined area. We couldn't work for money and we owned little to exchange for food. The Nazis wanted to starve us to death but we had other ideas.

"How did I feel at the time? What had I discovered so far? I learned to expect adversity with every breath. Tough times trained me. Simple as that. I became stronger and more confident of our chances to would make it through this ordeal. But every day brought challenges.

"Upon leaving our room each morning to find food, the same questions plagued me: *Would I see my family again? Could I steal enough wood to make a fire to warm what food scraps I could gather? Would I be caught by Nazis? Would I be shot?*

My Father, My Changes

"My father was the greatest human being that I ever met in my life. He taught me through his daily teaching to be an honorable man. I had such a learned father.

I spent hours with him as he taught me all he could about life. He explained how he felt not having a wife who had died earlier. My older brother died in my father's hands while saying his last prayers. My brother was a carbon copy of my father. He was an artist, a great Hebrew and a Talmud scholar. He got sent back from a camp after he had volunteered to return to the ghetto. It was a mistake. They meant to send him to a concentration camp but they brought him back to the ghetto. There was no means of saving him. He became too sick to take him out again and he died.

Widely respected, my father taught me to be an honest person, not a thief. But going into other people's bombed-out residences in search of survival necessities meant that I had to steal. I thought like a criminal would think. As is so often the case, desperate times called for desperate steps. What a conflicted situation it must have been for my father, a man of integrity with solid values. On one hand, he was hoping he raised me properly to never steal, but, at the end of the day, was thankful for what I brought home for our family through whatever means available. Basically, I had to do wrong to do right. There were days and nights I had to procure and steal, do whatever I could to live. I got wood, food, took houses apart to get a few lb. of wood so I could boil up a little water.'

"I developed a new set of standards because my simple earlier life had become complicated and unpredictable. As a student, I did my best to make my father proud of me. But moving into the ghetto brought a whole new way of life. Over time, ordinary events became unpredictable. My feelings had changed and my spirit was evolving. Thinking back some 70 years later, I can recall changes that were forced upon me due to circumstances:

"First, in my younger years, going to bed at night suggested I would enjoy a peaceful night's sleep with no unexpected sounds other than those associated with city life. But in the ghetto, the sounds changed to screams or shots as Jews were being killed.

"Next, going to school once meant getting an education from my teachers and spending time with my friends. But in the ghetto, the streets became my new teachers. I was forced into competition with thousands of other Jews for scraps of food, sticks to burn, anything to survive just one more day.

"Before the Germans' arrival, I often smiled but my smiles afterward were rare. Had I forgotten how? Rather than smiling, each moment was spent looking warily out of the sides of my eyes wishing I could see around corners to avoid potential dangers.

"Lastly, I remembered my father's calm and loving ways as he had taught me so much in my pre-ghetto days. His gentle ways were expressed through his calm voice and trusting, caring eyes. Father's eyes were such a contrast to the Nazi soldiers' eyes as they surely had targeted me through their rifles' scopes. I needed eyes everywhere. Outliving the horror meant learning, adjusting, and devising stratagems to get through each day.

The Ghetto Gets Crowded

"In the fall of 1941, we were shocked to see 20,000 more Jews from other parts of Poland transferred to our Lodz ghetto. Their arrival meant more mouths to feed with less food available. The newcomers appeared shocked to see our living conditions and they actually had more than we did. They got off the trains with shoes, clothes and even extra food! They looked in disbelief at our emaciated bodies as we stood before them wearing the same clothes we wore on our arrival almost two years earlier. It must be understood that there were too many frantic people jammed into small spaces. The newly arrived refuge families jockeyed for room, children cried and parents argued. They had been homeless for weeks. Many had walked hundred of miles to reach Warsaw, hoping for a bath or food. In the ghetto, they found neither.

"Shortly, the ghetto population grew even more when 5,000 gypsies were added to our living quarters. Not good neighbors, they stole and set fires to our area. Our bad living conditions worsened.

"The winter of 1941-42, when I was 14, was the most difficult. Coal and wood became harder to find. What little food there was had to be heated to become edible. The scarcity of fuel to heat food, along with frostbite, prevented many Jews from eating resulting in even more deaths.

"It was horrible watching the ghetto people in their clothes. Of course, many had lost so much weight due to malnutrition. Their clothes were stained as they had worn them through filthy conditions for long periods. They were bought during better times when they actually fit and now they fit like grain sacks on bony skeletal frames. Some people were so thin, even their socks wouldn't stand up! People wereeven starving to the point that it was impossible to judge people's ages.

Just to underscore the lack of food that Jews were permitted, I will provide some figures. In Warsaw, the Germans allowed themselves 2100 calories a day. The Polish were allowed 900 calories a day; but the daily ration for Jews was a mere 183 calories. Clearly, they planned for deliberate starvation.

The Ghetto Becomes Less Crowded

"Why? In early January of 1942, more deportations were planned for Chelmno. In less than two weeks, over 10,000 had been deported which continued until June of 1944. But every day a train left for a death camp, it was like a reprieve for the rest of us. It was safe to be in the street again for another day as we all struggled for food with fewer people to compete against. At the time, I was fifteen and getting skilled at ghetto survival.

"In early 1944, it was rumored the Russians were approaching Lodz and the Germans, becoming scared, decided to empty the ghetto. The Russians were close and we hoped for a miracle. Perhaps the Germans could then understand how we 80,000 to 90,000 remaining Jews had felt since the Nazis began occupying our city. It was doubtful there were that many Jews in one area anywhere in Europe at the time. What had become a makeshift life for us, as we knew it, was over. Our future became subject to rumor. The term 'resettled' was coupled with the phrase 'unknown destination.' 'Deportation' suggested our future was beyond our control. As the chaos increased, my confidence lessened with the uncertainty before us. I felt scared and insecure.

Hiding

"The Nazis went house to house, block by block, grabbing people at gunpoint. People were seized without discrimination to age, sex or family members. As long as they were Jews, nothing else mattered. Whole families were snatched and shipped away.

"But our family chose to buy time and hide. For me, it was not easy to continue knowing I was responsible for the rest of my family. The obligation fell upon me, like it or not, I accepted it. Today, my family members are not crying, not weeping. I hope they're praying for me somewhere but we don't know that.

"The Lodz ghetto had been split into three geographical groups for deportation purposes. Our group had to cross a bridge once our section was emptied out of Jews.

"As my father, sister and I crossed the bridge with other refugees we heard a familiar voice shout our names. It was my niece whom we hadn't seen in some time. She and my sister were close in age and good friends before the German invasion. We all lived in the ghetto, but seldom connected with each other. She invited us to stay with her on the other side of the ghetto. We agreed and slept the best we could on the floor.

"The next day, my father, sister and I searched for our own place. It was unwise to stay in one place more than one night. Luckily, we found an empty apartment which seemed to have been either abandoned by its owners or they had been snatched by the Nazis. Being empty, it met our meager needs, especially when my father saw potential hiding places in the attic.

"He pried open two boards in the attic's knee-wall and discovered enough space between the wall boards and the roof for us to hide. We wiggled our way through the opening and, upon Father's direction, pulled a portable coal stove in front of the boards. My clever father figured how to lean the stove against the boards effectively separating us from any Nazi searchers.

"While hiding in the attic, I saw many hidden odds and ends which others must have put in there. With little to do for three or four days, I found a diary of a girl. She recorded everything in her stay there which totaled hundreds of pages written in Polish. Sadly, I left it but wished I hadn't as it probably got burned when the ghetto was finally destroyed and the Nazis set it ablaze.

"Father had another strategy as he placed some food scraps on the table in that attic room. By doing so, it suggested people had been in the middle of a meal when they were surprised and grabbed by Nazi soldiers. Leftover food suggested there was no longer anyone there. Food being so scarce, would only be left behind if people were suddenly taken away. It worked several times as we heard soldiers running up the stairs with weapons drawn, only to find an empty room with partly eaten food on the table.

"It was frightening as we watched them through the wall's cracks. Motionless, we held our breaths and hoped our racing hearts were silent. The slightest sneeze, cough or growls from our empty stomachs could give us away. The Nazis sometimes sat for periods of time to rest as we remained perfectly still. Luckily, they had no dogs to detect our human scents. Those minutes seemed like hours as we waited for them to leave.

"When we exhausted all hiding places, it became obvious we had to turn ourselves in to the Nazis. We had no choice. It meant deportation on the train's cattle car. How were Jews selected? There was no system in place as the Germans were desperate. Some people volunteered hoping the Germans would let them stay together as a family but it was not a guarantee. It was just a matter of cleaning up the Jews. We hid until the arrival of the final transport. I often wonder what would have happened if we had stayed with the 800 Jews who remained behind to clean up the ghetto. But we'd made our decision to go.

"In August of 1944, we boarded that cattle car with about 80 other Lodz refugees. Where were we going? We had no idea except we were told we were going to an "unknown destination."

"We felt our lives were going to be over no matter where we went. The six extermination places for Jews existed only in Poland. The only reason they were in Poland was because the Polish people didn't mind it. The Polish people went to the places the trains would pass through and saw opportunities to make money with the poor physical condition we Jews were in. Many of us were dehydrated so the Jews were willing to trade their gold rings or watches for a glass of water!

"The conditions aboard the trains were horrible. Of course, there were no bathrooms which made it almost unbearable. The trains went slowly and many people were crying loudly because of the appalling surroundings. Someone rumored that they were going to gas us right in the cattle car.

"I remember one person fainting and someone nearby supplying them with ammonia. When the Jews smelled that distinct smell, they thought the gassing had already begun. Women were grabbing their children and holding their babies close by as chaos and commotion erupted. This complete disorder continued for many hours. Fortunately, we took along what we could and had managed to grab some bread before we left the ghetto. While on the way to Auschwitz, we saw some Jewish workers repairing roads and they kept asking us for bread with a warning that we wouldn't need it where we were going. We had figured that without them telling us.

Auschwitz

"We arrived in the afternoon. The train slowed down for the last ten miles going slower and slower until it finally stopped. I found out later why the train slowed down so early. It was because they were still gassing a previous trainload of Jews and they hadn't yet cleaned up the all corpses. We arrived late in the afternoon at this huge camp called Auschwitz. It was twenty-five square miles in size.

"The armed German guards, along with their fierce dogs, opened up the doors telling us to first throw down all of our possessions. We had little bags containing odds and ends but were not allowed to carry them off the train. All we had were our clothes on our backs.

"Jews came to help us off the train. Then our stuff was brought to giant warehouses which were called 'Canada.' They got that name because the Polish somehow thought that Canada was a country of great riches. Evidently, they felt our belongings were belongings of rich people. So untrue.

"We arrived at the ramp which emptied out to a selection man at the bottom. The first part of the process consisted of two orders, 'Women to the right!' and 'Men to the left!' Once separated, I saw my sister on the other side with the women while my father and I were together with the other males. My father had a rupture so he wore kind of a belt that held him up (and in) on that side of his body.

My sister spotted me in the line and kept yelling, 'Take care of Daddy! That's the last thing she ever said to me. We stayed in line and went through a further selection process. In that line, I became afraid for my father, so I remained about two or three spots behind him.

"I was afraid that he would make a bad decision which could cost us our lives. Essentially, I became my father's father and prepared myself to correct any decision he might make. At the bottom of the ramp was a man named Dr. Josep Mengele. I learned later just who he was.

As a historical reference, Dr. Mengele was a German SS officer and a physician in Auschwitz. He became infamous as the man who supervised the selection of arriving prisoners. It was he who determined who was to be killed immediately and who was to become a forced laborer. Mengele was also known for his medical experiments which performed without any form of anesthesia. He was particularly thrilled when he saw prisoners who were twins, especially children. He singled out twins to study if there was a way for Aryan women to be able to produce only blonde haired, blue-eyed children thus guaranteeing the Third Reich of eliminating everyone except those having such traits. He was called the "Angel of Death."

This infamous man was captured by the Americans and released before they realized who he was. By then, he had escaped eventually relocating to South America where he evaded capture for the rest of his life and died from a stroke while swimming in 1979.

"But back to the ramp: we filed down toward this man named Mengele who alone decided whether a person was sent to the right (for the sick, children or females) or to the left for men volunteering for 'hard work.'

My father, being forever the intellectual, stops at Mengele's desk and begins talking with him using his flawless German. I jumped up a few spaces to be with my father and said quickly, 'Don't talk!' But he continues to talk and Mengele asked my father his age. Father answered "Forty-four.'

Mengele demanded to see his papers verifying his age so Father heads back toward the train. I caught up with him asking, 'Father, what did you do? What are you going to do?'

He answered, 'I am going to show him my papers.'

I responded, 'There's a mountain of stuff back there that people threw away. How are you going to find your bag? There are 2,000 packages there. How are you going to find your papers?'

I convinced him to go back into the line and suggested that Mengele might not recognize him from before. I insisted my father turn left at the table. But then Father started arguing with me saying we should go to the other side because that would be easier work. I corrected him saying,

'Don't go where there is easy work. Go where there is hard work.'

"I figured out that if you went to the easy work line, that meant death, not easy work. Hard work meant life, at least temporarily. He listened. Mengele had a cane with a curved crook at the end so he could hook someone around the neck who went the wrong way and yank them back to the other line. He never got the chance to use the hook on my father as Mengele had moved on to the next person.

"My father and I were transferred several times to different camps including one of the primary killing camps named Birkenau. The Germans were in a hurry to avoid the quickly approaching Russians. Along with my father, I kept volunteering for hard work, regardless of our physical condition.

"Appearing eager to work may just have saved our lives. As it turned out, I was returned to Auschwitz after narrowly missing several gas chamber lineups in other camps. I was there just before the famous uprising by the prisoners in Auschwitz which happened in early October of 1944. Some of the prisoners assigned to help with the cremation destroyed one of the crematoriums and a gas chamber using explosives which were smuggled into the camp by women who worked outside the camp. The uprising was put down easily by the SS. Shortly after, I was transferred again.

"The Russians liberated Auschwitz on January 27, in 1945. By then, there were only 7,500 prisoners remaining as 60,000 had been taken on forced death marches before the Russians arrived. During the war, Auschwitz with its surrounding camps, had killed more that 1 million people. When the Russians arrived, they found thousands of emaciated prisoners and piles of corpses left behind.

"My father and I survived the war and happily connected months later after a brief separation. It was a joyous occasion despite losing our family members earlier.

"My life then had been redirected so many times causing me to find new ways to help our family. It was all part of my growth and, in the end, I was spared for a reason: to share my eyewitness accounts of what happened in that horrific period.

"As you can see, these pages provided a glimpse of how 'I grew up fast.' As my years went by I evolved into an even more loving son, a stronger Jew, and a person who believed that only death destroys hope. My requirement to lived called for action without delay. That preparedness was important to our well-being. As I reflect upon those years, the changes in my spirit and maturity have led to a deeper connection with my Jewish heritage.

"I am thrilled with the opportunity to capture these events just as my father had hoped."

As I wrote, and re-wrote David's story, my eyes well up as if I were slicing an onion, no matter how many times I go over it. I feel that following the Holocaust, all other tragedies ranked far behind on a misery scale. I wondered many times of the thousands, perhaps millions, of others to whom this story happened, whose narratives will never be shared and appreciated. My hope is that David's story will stand for many others who could have told comparable stories if their fate took them down a less fortunate road. I so hope the readers can appreciate with gratitude the lives they lead today based on David's story.

This story, although longer than the ones that preceded it, is a story of either learning to adjust or perishing. That phrase, to a lesser extent, is a lesson which can apply to all of us no matter our current plight in life.

We return now to a much lighter note following the heavier-than-normal discussion on the Holocaust as we now listen to Freeman Leonard ("In The Beginning . . . Alpha") when he describes running films between the Vineyard towns. Because of national security, most of the east coast of America was either in a "brownout" or "blackout" status. Freeman explains it well below.

1943-45
Blackout, Brownouts & Movies

"The island rotation of America's movies over a year's time was quite involved. We'd try to get the recent highly-rated movies early in the summer but were forced to take the 'also-rans' in the winter when our island population had fewer people. We tried this same rotation between the towns during World War II which called for some clever driving.

"When I drove the movie reels to Edgartown during the war, it proved difficult. During the war, there was strict gas rationing for cars which called for a certain sticker. An 'A' sticker meant that the driver was allotted only three gallons of gas a week. I don't remember the limits of a 'B' sticker but it meant that you were permitted to buy slightly more gas than the 'A' sticker. The 'C' sticker, on the other hand, meant that one was entitled to an almost unlimited supply of gas per week. Fortunately, I was given the highly sought after 'C' sticker.

"The reason for the 'C' sticker? The rationing people felt that my job of driving the films considered necessary to improve morale of our island's citizens during wartime. Diversions were seen as a major benefit for those left behind to run the homes and families. It was helpful that my C sticker had a stamp on it which read 'Projectionist.'

"We, on the Vineyard, were 'blacked out' for military purposes. This meant no lights were allowed on at night which could provide possible bombing targets for our enemies. On the Vineyard, like most east coast towns and cities, there were air-raid wardens hired to check each neighborhood ensuring all people were following the prescribed degree of darkness. Americans became deeply connected with this program. By

1943, there were six million volunteers serving in some capacity in public protection. A 'blackout' differed from a 'brownout.' A brownout meant that house lights may be left on but all shades had to be drawn to reduce the visible light. The blackout meant, in addition, that no cars were to be driven with their headlights on.

"In fact, there were scheduled and advertised air raid drills throughout our coastlines where the street lights were shut off at a certain time. People outdoors were to take cover inside the nearest building. Blinds were pulled and inside lights were turned way down. The theory was that enemy pilots couldn't bomb if they couldn't spot targets.

"I recall something businesses in New Jersey were reluctant to shut down their lights during these times as doing so would cut into their business. But it is easy to understand why both enemy submarines and planes would prefer the lights to be on to better pinpoint targets.

"The blackout concept was necessary as our leaders had no time to prepare for a large-scale attack from either Germany or Japan and our citizens were nervous about the unknown. Our government decided that if Americans could take steps to protect themselves, they would feel both safer and directly involved in the war effort.

"During a blackout period, I was granted permission to drive on the Beach Road to deliver the movies but had to do so with my lights off. When I drove Beach Road, if the moon was shining and my lights were out, I couldn't tell the road from the beach. Everything looked the same.

"This trip became my nightly challenge. I drove my 1936 Oldsmobile between all three towns with my lights turned off. At the time, there were military people stationed on the island to practice training maneuvers. These men proved to be most accommodating to me, especially when their large amphibious landing 'Ducks' practiced landings on the Beach Road. I was often caught in the middle of their caravans as I drove between towns.

"I was caught, the first time, by the golf course. They weren't aware of my special Civil Defense authorization and I had to explain. Following my explanation, they became helpful and often jumped on my car's running board to got me past other military personnel. After a while, they expected me at predictable times.

"It became quite easy, after many nights' practice, to drive with no headlights. Fortunately, I knew most of the roads, but, when in doubt, I rigged a small spotlight which cast a beam as big around as your finger. It safely guided me along the side of the road. The light was not as bright as a lit cigarette so the island's safety wasn't jeopardized. It wasn't difficult driving although I certainly couldn't see other cars in the road. Fortunately, there were few cars out as they needed special permission. Another factor in there being fewer cars was the rubber shortage during the war. Tires were hard to buy. During the war, many cars were placed on blocks."

———————

Below is a brief account of America doing its part to help out the war effort. It is told in Gene Seaman's memoir titled "Light and Life" as she recalled her younger married years in Washington, D. C.

1944
Victory Gardens

During the war, resources of all kinds were being diverted to support the war effort. It resulted in American citizens planting "Victory Gardens" which came in all shapes and sizes. We all worked the soil to raise food for families, friends, and neighbors. Our Washington gardens were viewed as both family and community efforts and were never considered drudgery. They were viewed more as a pastime and national duty. Even Claude Wickard, the Secretary of Agriculture who lived on the same street as we did throughout the war, had his own beautiful victory garden.

———————

Ralph Brown, from his memoir titled "Truly Blessed" spent several years in the military both during WW II and later served a stint in the Korean War. He shares with us his experiences in the Pacific theater.

1941-1945
The Pacific Theater

"From California, I was sent to Honolulu where we stayed under rather crude conditions on the left shore of the entrance to Honolulu Harbor. We were given temporary assignments in the Communications Headquarters at the Naval Air Station and within three weeks were transferred there to a permanent station with excellent living quarters on the Bachelor's Office Quarters. This important and interesting work was done mostly at night. I played tennis days as the climate was wonderful. What a break!

"Following the devastating attack on Pearl Harbor, the Japanese quickly succeeded in capturing some Pacific Islands in the Western Pacific which, if controlled by the U. S., could be used as stepping stones to the Japanese mainland.

"The first islands that had to be re-taken by America were the Marshalls and the Gilberts. The distance was so great that a fueling station was necessary between them and Honolulu. There was an atoll called Johnson Island mostly covered by water that had served as a bird sanctuary. It was about 800 miles west of Honolulu. Engineering expertise enlarged this land to about the size of a large aircraft carrier. A fueling station was created there so the flights could be made to the Marshalls and Gilberts. After bitter fighting at Kuajalein, these islands were re-taken. They could now proceed to retake the Mariannas, Tinian, Guam and Saipan, Iwo Jima, and then continue on toward Japan.

"We in intelligence knew sometimes of the Japanese command's strategies and intentions through our decoding work. This knowledge not only helped us prevent military disasters but allowed us to win decisive sea battles and recapture precious islands as stepping stones for an eventual attack on Japan.

Saipan

"My commanding officer made the necessary arrangements to have me transferred. I immediately felt better about being able to contribute more directly. I was heading to Saipan, one of the three Marianas Islands which had just been re-taken from the Japs by our forces.

"What an odd set of circumstances followed me during the war as I prepared for my new job. The original intent was to have me serve as a landing ship officer to a gunnery crew on transports then into communications in Hawaii and finally to a squadron in Saipan. Our headquarters were in a former Japanese seaplane base and my role would be as a communications officer involved in the transport of all items across the Pacific.

"When I arrived in Saipan I was with what they called the Naval Air Transport Service or 'NATS' (Naval Air Transport Squadron) as it was called. We flew four engine seaplanes called Coronadoes. They were very slow and only capable of 110 knots. We flew going westerly at 8000 feet and on return trips at 7000 feet. These planes were not even pressurized so we couldn't go to higher elevations.

"To make matters even more perilous, we weren't armed. Without question, we were sitting ducks. They were hardly crafts of comfort as they weren't insulated with anything but packing blankets hanging loosely on the side of the fuselage. When flying, we'd be in temperatures so cold that we needed layers of clothing covered with a flight jacket. When we landed on some of the islands we'd be facing temperatures of 105' or more! Temperature extremes were tough on our systems.

"To add to the discomfort, we had to cope with the landings. The seaplanes had no wheels . . . only flotations. Landing was a lengthy operation leaving many of us nauseous by the time we got off. The planes carried about fifteen passengers along with air mail and as many supplies as possible from the states. Most items came by ship. I remember once getting some cookies by ship from my wife back home. By the time they arrived, they were so hard they were not edible. I recall the only way to get them down was by sucking on them. Nonetheless, they were so good and we all enjoyed them.

"Let me tell you, this place wasn't all that safe from the Japanese and although we had overtaken the island from the enemy, about twenty-one of them remained hiding high in the cliffs and hills. As you know, they were fanatical in their loyalty and dying didn't mean that much to them. Their country came first. Anywhere you went off base you ran the risk of being picked off by a sniper. One always had to be alert.

"From our base, we could look up high in the cliffs and see where the American troops had used flamethrowers to force them out of those caves. The face of the cliffs was all black and charred. I'd guess many never made it out and just died in there. There is no way they could have possibly survived. As a 29-year-old Edgartown boy, I had a difficult time understanding the violence that had taken place but, at the same time, I had no sympathy for the Japanese after what they had done to us.

"We lived in tents that were about four to five feet above the ground because the rain came so heavily it came down almost in sheets as if each drop was connected to another. We could take our showers right out in the rain while collecting rainwater in our steel helmets for shaving. The rainwater was also drained off the tent roofs which we used for washing and brushing our teeth.

"The Japanese tower was still left from their original air base. There were pill boxes everywhere covered up by earth so the remains of recent battles were visible. On this island you could walk out for several thousand feet offshore and not even be up to your knees with water. You see, the islands were on coral reefs and volcanic ash. Along the way one could pick up many beautiful varieties of shells. The downside of the walk out in the water was, on occasion, viewing some of the human remains from the earlier battles for Saipan.

"The famous actor, Tyrone Power, had also been shipped to Saipan. On occasion, he served as a pilot with our Air Command. While stationed there his transport squadron carried supplies to the advancing forces. He, too, chose this duty and remained there until the end of the war.

"About 1000 B-29s left daily around noon from Tinian, Guam and Saipan. The planes used in this role were originally B-17's but were replaced by the larger B-29's. Each was loaded with 500 lb. jelly bombs. These bombs weren't necessarily explosive but were designed to create fire. On impact, these powerful bombs landed and set long-lasting fires to all the surrounding areas. You see, the buildings in Japan were made of highly flammable materials and were poorly defended. Our bombing raids in Germany at the same time were less effective as their buildings were much stronger being made of masonry.

"During my career, before the dropping of the atomic bomb, I'd seen the results of these jelly bombs in Tokyo and other major Japanese cities. Literally, whole sections of the city were completely burned out. All you could see was bare ground. It was so terribly devastating that I could never understand how the Japs could continue fighting. After two months of bombing their large cities, we started on their smaller cities. They had millions of homeless citizens yet they still didn't surrender. Our goal was to immobilize their home islands and cities before the land invasion started. Again, they were so loyal to their country's causes that they'd undergo almost any sacrifice rather than surrender.

"There was an island chain east of us called 'Truk' which was actually a series of small islands. The Japs were rooted in deeply them along with their bottled-up naval ships. They just couldn't' move. Our planes circled back after a successful bombing run once they'd run out of targets. They mercilessly dropped extra bombs on Truk. The area was filled with sunken ships which had been bottled up there with no chance to escape. I have no idea how any of them survived. After viewing the widespread devastation I was lost for words to describe the carnage.

"An interesting sidelight . . . Yes, I heard the famous broadcaster Tokyo Rose taunting us daily with her repeated pleas for the Americans to give up the fight and return home to their wives. I admit she had a very soothing voice that would almost melt you. In all honesty, it had no impact on me other than disdain. As far as I was concerned, what they had done to us in Pearl Harbor far outweighed any small amount of sympathy I might have had. Even to this day, I would never buy a Japanese car even if it meant that I never had a car. I wouldn't do it, that's all. Most of my family has one but not this old boy!

Okinawa

"They made their last stand in Okinawa and I want to tell you that it was a hellhole beyond words. We lost many men, ships, and planes but it turned out to be one of the major turning points of the entire war. The shame of it is that this island was one of the most beautiful islands in the Pacific. It was midway between Manila (in the Philippines) and Tokyo. The Japs didn't want to give it up because it was so strategically important and was the first Japanese land invaded. The American commanders underestimated the numbers of defenders and their superb organization on Okinawa.

"The Americans had a fairly easy time landing on shore but ran into real trouble once they tried to advance past the Jap defensive lines. It took six days of fighting just to get past them. In the meantime, our fleet of ships was getting pounded by the Japs' air force especially with suicide ("kamikaze") attacks which killed 5,000 American sailors. The Japanese fought fiercely as they were pushed right to the last edge of the island. Rather than be taken prisoners and surrender, many of the soldiers chose to jump off high cliffs to their deaths. They just hated the concept of surrender and would never allow themselves to be taken prisoner. That's why over so many American prisoners were found killed on the sides of the road during the Death March of Bataan in the Philippines.

"We lost 50,000 and the enemy lost 117,000 on Okinawa. In the meantime, Manila had been taken by the Japs and then re-taken by us. During the fighting at Okinawa, we evacuated many of our most seriously wounded back to Manila. I remember seeing men come back from that battle who had actually turned gray. I had a chance to visit the major city of Naha, Okinawa and it was a disaster.

Hiroshima & Nagasaki

"In early August of 1945, we dropped the atomic bomb on Hiroshima and then Nagasaki. It's interesting to note that had we not dropped the bomb, the Japs were about to be destroyed by our planned massive invasion called 'Operation Downfall' which I mentioned earlier. It involved a major attack by land at several key strategic positions at the same time. This would have incapacitated most all of Japan's capabilities. The downside of such an attack meant an estimated loss of thousands of American soldiers. It was decided to drop the bomb. Let me tell you, with or without the atomic bomb, Japan was about to be soundly defeated.

"The bomb destroyed 80% of Hiroshima's buildings and killed an estimated 70,000 people. Sixteen hours after the bomb was dropped President Truman contacted the Japanese government and told them to surrender or face a 'rain of ruin' from the air. They didn't respond, a big mistake. As promised, two days later, Nagasaki was flattened. This time over 100,000 people either were killed, injured or simply vanished.

"We didn't know it but one of our neighboring islands called Tinian, in the Marianas, was the takeoff area for the strike. A secret America strike force had been training in Utah and in Cuba. They kept practicing the same mission: the dropping of a single 10,000 lb. bomb precisely on a target. It worked and peace finally settled over the world.

"During the war, I often looked at my situation and reflected upon it. I still do as I tell my experiences. There were times that I felt I would have been just as well off if I'd kept my mouth shut about getting out there close to the action. But then I had to live with myself. That first sickness in my stomach when hearing of Edmund Berube's death stayed with me. The idea that I improve my efforts toward shortening the war has really stuck with me. There were many chances to compare my situation with others during the war and I must say that mine, indeed, was a picnic. Oh, sure, I was still in danger of not returning but, as always, the unknown is part of life. There was that one word . . . 'uncertainty.'

"It was a key word. I remember it as one of the most difficult concepts of the war. How long was it going to last? Was I going to be there forever? Would I ever get back to my beloved family and our home in Arlington that I missed so much? The mental strain of it all was as tough as the physical discomforts we all faced. As it turned out, I was there for about a year and a half until the end of the war.

I'm proud to say I was there when one of our squadron's planes flew Admiral Nimitz to Tokyo for the signing of the peace treaty aboard the battleship Missouri. As I watched him board the plane I felt it was finally over. The Japanese government ceased to be run by its military leaders and a new Cabinet was to be installed for their rebuilding. General MacArthur took over and the Japanese surrender was unconditional.

"In all honesty, I must say I didn't actually participate physically in any of the combat that I've described as I was somewhat safely ensconced in Saipan. Occasionally, I got out closer to the action to do something associated with my work in communications and again when I made a trip to Shang-Hai near the end of my Pacific tour.

"When returning from Shang-Hai, I remember a scene which will be forever etched in my mind. We looked out the windows at the plane's wings and saw all four engines were overheated. Each was a fiery red-hot color which was not all that uncommon. We then hit an air pocket. The navigator hit his head on the roof receiving a bad injury. It was so scary! *Was I about to die?*

"It was a frightening time when it was only natural to wonder if this would serve as the end for me just before I finally was heading home.

"We somehow made it safely to ground. Our plane was badly damaged and never flew again. It wasn't worth fixing and that style of plane was outdated. The modern planes were much faster and more versatile."

We'll now return to the European Theater through the story about Arden Schofield, a family cousin. These are his actual words which he wrote and was included in my recently published book, "Our Final Salute."

My Story

by
Arden Schofield

"My story which I now relate is true and quite eventful.

"I went to England in November 1944 with our artillery company of the 106th Division which had been activated in 1943. After having been in England for a few weeks, Chaplain Mark Moore, with whom I was assigned, was making plans with our artillery commander as to our proceeding to France.

"We crossed the English Channel and arrived in Roveri, France. As we traveled in our jeep through the country, we saw much destruction, but the people were very joyful. They had already been liberated from the Germans. Germany had been occupying France since 1940. It was now 1944—four long years. Our trip through France was now coming to an end.

"We would soon be approaching St. Vith, Belgium, not too far from the German border. There was now a feeling that the war would soon be over. From June 1944 to December 1944, there had been a sense of quietness, but that was not to last.

"On Saturday morning, December 16, 1944 about five o'clock, all hell broke loose. The German were firing their shells into the town of St. Vith, Belgium, where we were. The Battle of the Bulge had now begun. Chaplain Moore thought that we should now go into Germany to be with our artillery troops. We left St. Vith for Germany thinking that we would return to St. Vith, but that was not to be.

"We were trapped. As we drove around in Germany, we happened to spot an old church. When we got out of the jeep, we met a Captain Pitts. The captain was looking for a place to have services for his men. In the church, we saw the organ. The captain now wanted to hear it. We first examined it to be sure that it wasn't mined. Then I turned the organ on, after which I played a few hymns for the captain as well as for Chaplain Moore.

"A few days later we learned that Captain Pitts had died. We were given permission to go and bring his remains back for a Christian burial. His death turned out to be our first casualty. I have felt so happy that I had played some hymns on that organ for the captain.

"We finally left the church only to realize that we were still in Germany and lost. Now our problems seemed to magnify. To be confined in a foreign country was not our goal. Back into the jeep we went. We now resumed our search to find our way out of the country.

"On the following Tuesday, after having been riding all around, we came to a hill. The Germans knew exactly where we were. Now they began firing their shells into our area. Our commander now realized that our troops were in serious trouble. At that point, many of the German troops came towards us with their burp guns. We were so surprised when we noticed that some of these soldiers looked so young. Now we were prisoners of war—prisoners of the Germans.

"We had to march for a few days in the Ardennes forest. It was bitterly cold with snow added to our problems. To drop to the ground from sheer exhaustion, while on the march was not to be tolerated. We could be shot.

"After many miles on the march, we finally arrived at a railroad station, in front of which were many boxcars, much smaller than in our country. On the sides of these small cars, in French, were the words 40 hommes—men or 8 chevaux—horses could well fit. Well over 50 of us men were crammed into these small cars. All that we were given to eat was a biscuit.

"Then the box car doors were slammed tight, there was no light. Everything became a shadow. There were no toilet facilities. One can almost imagine what the conditions were like. During the night the RAF would bomb the marshaling yards. We could hear the whistling, screeching sound of the bombs on their way down. The bombs hit nearby causing our car to rock on the tracks. 'The Lord's Prayer' was said many, many times. It was a most terrible sensation. I feel certain that the RAF did not know that we were prisoners of war in these boxcars. But that was war. They had a job to fulfill.

"After the RAF left the scene, the German guard opened the box car doors to let us out. I should say—let us fall out. Some of us were in a weakened condition. Now we really needed water. The only water we received was from the snow on the ground.

"We got back into the box cars hoping that the RAF would not return. After a few more days, we arrived in the town of Bad Orb, Germany. Many of the citizens came down to the station to stare at us. We asked them for wasser (water). Most of them turned a deaf ear to our request. The German Commander then called our names out. We had to listen carefully for the pronunciations. It took about 2 or 3 hours in the cold.

"When the roll call was completed, we had to march up a very steep hill, fighting the cold wind. We were very tired, but we still could not fall to the ground. There was always the fear of being shot. However, we did make the final ascent. I still don't know how we did it—but we did.

"The facilities at Stalag 1XB Bad Orb were atrocious. The toilet situation was very far from being acceptable. It has been stated that Stalag

1XB was the worst prisoner of war camp in Germany. We could attest to that.

"t wasn't very long before I came down with the worst condition concerning the terrible effects of dysentery. Being in captivity, there certainly was no medication. Believe me; I was in a complete terrible state. The food at noon was one piece of bread with some watery soup. The worst soup was called Green Hornet or Green Death. It was made from everything that was green. There were also pine needles in the soup. We had to bite them in half or they would gag us as they were going down. Each man's bowl of soup had an ample supply of little white worms. There was certainly no meat shortage in that soup.

"We never took our clothes off except when the guards took us to have a shower. It would take me almost 40 minutes to strip down. I now looked at my body for the first time in months. I couldn't believe what I saw. I had sores all over my body. There was also an abundance of lice in my mop of hair. Then I started to put my clothes back on. It took me longer to dress. In my weakened condition it consumed a great deal of effort, which I was somewhat lacking.

"As the months went by, General George Patton was forging his way through Germany. God bless that wonderful man. He had liberated more prisoners of war prisons than any other officers.

"Good Friday, April 1945, General Patton's soldiers broke through the prison gate. I knew where I was. I was lying on the barracks floor. I couldn't get up. I did notice that some of those wonderful soldiers had tears in their eyes. It seemed that they couldn't believe what they had seen.

"One of the patients who was here at Liberty Commons by the name of Dick Sorenson had been in General Patton's army. I most certainly believe that Dick had contributed in some way to my liberation. Dick has since passed away. Dick, may you rest in peace. I will never forget you. God Bless you!

"The medical people came in immediately and took care of the worst cases. I was one of them. Easter morning was truly my day of resurrection. I was flown to another hospital in Paris where I had further treatment.

"In Paris, there was another patient in the bed next to mine who was eating a hamburger. I asked him if he would order one for me. The final result was disastrous. It certainly didn't make me feel that great. My stomach was not quite ready for solid foods. My diet would have to stick with the soft foods for awhile. I still had dysentery. It remained with me for some time. The nurse would check my weight quite often. When I was in the prisoner of war Stalag 1XB in Bad Orb, Germany, I had lost a considerable amount of weight. I was told that once the dysentery had disappeared, things would be much better.

"One day an officer had come to my bed and told me that I was going home. He asked me how I wanted to travel. I told him the quickest way. I was taken to the airport in Paris where Charles Lindberg had landed in 1927 after his historic flight from New York.

"I was flown with some other patients to New York. When my litter was lowered to the ground, I reached over and picked up a handful of good American dirt and I swallowed it. I had lost my freedom and now I had regained it.

"Over the years I have given much thought about my experience. I have come to the conclusion that I am glad that I had gone through those adventurous months and survived. I think that it has made me a better person to love and to be loved.

"The chaplain with whom I had worked was truly a wonderful man. He and I were like buddies. Not too long ago I got a call from Kansas City. It was from a relative of Chaplain Mark Moore. He proceeded to tell me that Mark had passed away.

"I will *never, never* forget that good man.'"

The following story about Arden is from a book I recently wrote titled "Our Final Salute."

"In addition to Arden's own words, I had the good fortune to not only meet Arden, but speak with him of his WW II experiences. Our talks, coupled with research, gave me a basic knowledge for which I will be forever grateful. He shared much with me and now I am honored to share with my readers. The following is additional information, with time frames, to help sort out just what was happening in the war along with Arden's personal experiences:

Mid-December, 1944
Germany

"At that point in the war, a series of unfortunate events had merged for the Allied forces in Germany. First of all, they experienced a 'slowdown' in both travel and receiving supplies. On top of that, the Germans, especially Hitler, felt they had one great last offensive in them. Thirdly, some of the Allied troops were either battle weary or 'newbies' fresh off the boat assuming the war had been won.

"Arden's improvised organ recital, per request of Captain Pitts, was to be his last chance for some time to experience such a peaceful moment with his music.

"During this peaceful solitude, another soldier named was Dick Sorenson (whom he mentioned in his writing) was marching with General Patton toward the Ardennes Mountains in an effort to protect them from German attack. As an aside, I found it intriguing that *Arden* Schofield would be involved in the *Arden*nes Mountains. That name, with its dual linkage, would not be easily forgotten.

"This particular section of the Ardennes Mountain range was felt to be strategically critical. Why? Four years earlier, the French had overlooked protecting this area with adequate manpower. At that time, Hitler won a major battle against France's undermanned French forces.

"But that December, the Allied troops were stretched a bit thin yet their military leadership felt only minimal troops would be capable of defending that section of the mountain range against German aggression. But that proved untrue.

"A force of about 250,000 battle-tested German soldiers went up against the 80,000 Allied forces giving them over a 3-1 numerical advantage. The Allied troops were both outnumbered and under-equipped. With superior numbers, the Germans initiated the attack at about five o'clock. That was the beginning of the Germans punching a hole through that north-south line of weakened forces within the Ardennes Mountains. It produced a 'bulge' eastward extending about 50 miles deep and 70 miles wide. This offensive began on December 16, 1945 and was thereafter always known as 'The Battle of the Bulge.'

"This so called 'bulge' was temporary as the Germans could go no further for several reasons. First of all, the Americans, though outnumbered, delayed the German advance at key crossroads such as St. Vith and Bastogne. The Germans couldn't get around the American forces right away, but, as Arden will attest, they did so later.

"Secondly, the bulge got a bit crowded being a scant fifty miles wide. It squeezed many German vehicles and troops into a small area. But the Germans fought on. The cold and relentless snow which had fallen before, and after, the battle added to their problems. The Allied forces resisted this German offensive in southern Belgium and Luxembourg. Yet the Germans fought on to the point where they were eventually able to overpower sections of the Allied forces, even in St. Vith at Arden's location.

Captured!

"On December 16, 1944, Arden was in the middle of all that white fallen (and falling) snow when the German Army surprised the American and British troops by sneaking up on them in wearing white uniforms. The camouflage worked perfectly for the Germans as Arden explained to me:

'Jay, they rose up right out of the snow. Given that we were so completely surrounded, our artillery commander thought it would be best for us to surrender. At the time, I looked around and considered our alternatives; there were none. He made the right choice.'

"The Germans knew although they had won this battle, but were losing the war. It was time for them to run hard, away from advancing American troops. Arden, along with other prisoners, had no choice but to be swept along with their captors as they were marched through the forests to a train. Stuffed into freight cars, they were brought to German prisons with little water or food, and certainly no sanitary bathrooms in which to relieve themselves. Once this group of prisoners arrived in camp, they hoped in vain such conditions would improve. The Germans likely realized that with the Americans chasing them that hard, their prisoners would die. There would be all the fewer they'd have to move to the next camp, or 'stalag.'

"Above and beyond those horrible travel conditions, Arden added the winter of 1944-45 was "the coldest of the century."

1945
American Soldiers as German POWs

"I once heard a similar story of a group of American P.O.W.s who were being marched to another stalag in Mooseberg, Germany. Forced to sleep on the snow-covered ground, the men were just miserable. Throughout the march, American planes mistakenly strafed them killing many GIs. For some reason, the Germans allowed this group of POWs to stop on a hill for a religious service for President Roosevelt who had just died. The men, not wanting to be strafed again by American troops, took action.

"With toilet paper, they spelled out 'P-O-W' down the hill signaling that American troops were there. During the prayer service, one of the soldiers noticed some goats were eating their toilet paper warning. He ran down the hill chasing them away while his buddies laughed sharing the usual American humor, regardless of circumstances.

"Once they reached Mooseberg the prisoner count was so high that the POWs had to sleep in tents on ground, not in prison barracks as expected. To preserve body warmth, they slept close together ('cuddling') to avoid freezing to death. The men subsisted with German-provided 'Green' soup (soup contents with only green items such as grass and pine needles) and received Red Cross packages. Without those packages, many POWs would have died. But the Germans were also hungry which gave our resourceful American prisoners an idea.

"They offered their German captors some of their Red Cross parcels in exchange for materials and parts enabling some radio-savvy American soldiers to build a crystal radio. With those radios, they kept abreast of the war's progress, including General Patton's crossing of the Rhine River. They knew Americans were headed their way which inspired them to carry on no matter if food, water and shelter were low or even that local goats were eating their warning signs.

"Shortly afterwards, General Patton's Third Army arrived and liberated them. Within hours, these men was taken to a local air field for transport to hospitals. But at the air field, they saw an interesting sight. A few light planes arrived while carrying German officers who had fled to avoid capture by the approaching Russians. Germans much preferred surrendering to the civilized Americans rather than face the revenge-charged Russians.

Arden's Prison Conditions

"Arden related that Stalag 1XB Bad Orb was verified as Germany's worst POW camp. The town, located 30 miles northwest of Frankfurt, held French, Italian, Serbian, Russian and American P.O.W.s. Although all troops were severely mistreated, according to eyewitness accounts, the Russians were set aside for the worst treatment and were buried in mass graves. Bad Orb held almost 5,000 American P. O.W.s—far more than it was equipped to handle. The terrible food was rationed in insufficient quantities.

"In each barracks the 160 men prisoners were given no soap or towels to use the water tap with only cold water. There was a hole in the floor for a toilet, and the barracks were so overcrowded that the prisoners had to take turns sleeping with such limited floor space. There were no beds and even the mattresses in the camp's hospital were made of lice-infested straw.

"Somehow, Arden kept himself barely alive despite poor nourishment and unsanitary conditions. Those two factors contributed to most POWs deaths. During his five month imprisonment, he lost 80 pounds, from his six-foot tall body. It was not uncommon then for American prisoners to lose 100 lb. in 100 days! Arden shared with me the following story:

"'The skin just seemed to disappear from my bones. I remember being so hungry that when a bone became available to me I chewed on it like a dog would. Food became so important to me, especially all those foods I strongly craved. I kept a battered mess kit which I had found earlier at the prison camp. Slowly starving, I kept inside that kit dozens of pieces of paper on which I had written, lists of those foods I dreamed about.

"My list included 30 different kinds of meat—boiled ham, minute steak, corned beef, smoked ham, meatloaf, pork sausage, hamburger. Potatoes—mashed, boiled, buttered, sweet, creamed, french fries. Fruits—apples, oranges, apricots, prunes. Candy—chocolate, fudge, caramels, butternut fudge, taffy, and peanut brittle.'

"Arden continued, *There were no warm clothes, very little food and even less hope. Sadly, I watched many of my buddies die of malnutrition and various sicknesses.'* I bet he wondered just how, and when, it would all end for him. We will soon find out . . .

1945
General Patton's Path Through France & Germany

"Throughout the early spring of 1945, General Patton's Third Army pushed the Germans back through France and deep into Germany. Along with killing the enemy, American soldiers remained hopeful of finding, and possibly liberating, any Allied POWs still kept in German prison camps. This race against time drove them onward. They remained confident the Germans were kept on the run in a totally defensive, all-out retreating posture. As the weeks dragged by, Arden, although failing, stayed alive.

"For five months before April, Arden felt each day he was nearing his life's end. He had wasted away from several months of dysentery, the biting cold, and the ravaging hunger which all combined to signal his brain he had only a few days before death arrived removing all the pain he'd endured. But he might not have been aware that April 1st was approaching; that singularly American traditional holiday which brings all kinds of tricks and surprises for unsuspecting friends and family. I'm not sure of the 'trick' part of it but the Germans were certainly in for the surprise of their lives when General Patton's troops burst into the camp. Arden explained to me his joy better than I ever could when he told me,

'I was lying on my back on that wooden floor of that flimsy, dark building. I couldn't walk or even stand up. There were few muscles left to support even my 80 pounds. I couldn't see what was going on but could certainly hear it as Patton's men burst into our barracks. I recognized the new voices as American and soon understood what was happening. I just sort of smiled feeling reassured I had a real chance for survival. I couldn't believe it.'

"At that point, during his smile of appreciating God and all that He'd brought him, he remembered looking up to see a group of fellow Americans staring down at him with tears in their eyes. They were Americans, guaranteeing him freedom. The emotions of that moment etched forever in Arden's brain the sensation of living as he was meant to. He felt it indescribable and that it should never be taken for granted by any American. But even more feelings awaited Arden.

"Following this liberation, Arden and his fellow POWs were flown to Paris. He explained his physical condition upon his release:

'I'll never forget, I could hardly walk. They deloused us and I couldn't get my clothes off because they had been on so long, that they'd become stuck to my skin.

'When they finally lowered by litter, my stretcher, onto American soil for the first time, I scooped a handful of dirt and ate it, that's how grateful I was.'

"Shortly after, he was transported to Fort Devens beginning the long road toward recovery.

"At 93, Arden died on May 25, 2011, just a few weeks after I had sent him his chapter from the book, "Our Final Salute." Thanks, Arden, for all you gave us."

Now, for a brief contribution from Gene Seamans from her life story, "Light & Love." She speaks from the time she was nine years old. Her mother's sister married a man who would later be known as General George Patton. Gene loved her 'Uncle Georgie' and remembers an incident.

"The Pattons spent their time with us over most holidays, especially Thanksgiving. When he left the room every once in a while he went to the bathroom but always left the door open. When I was nine, I remember walking by the bathroom one time and he was standing in front of the bathroom mirror making all kinds of mean faces. He was evidently practicing for his speeches which later made him famous. I thought it was funny to see those faces he made when he normally was not like that."

We now return to Mr. Athanas, the charming Greek immigrant we met earlier. He describes an incident which happened to him in 1945 in New York City which told of a most interesting follow-up.

1945
New York City

"In 1945, I was walking on St. Nicholas Avenue in New York City, heading back to our apartment. There were many people walking on the sidewalk and I paid little attention to them. Someone walked past, recognized me, and shouted in a strong voice,

"'Teacher! Teacher! Teacher!'

"I thought it must have been either a current or former student who had recognized me and wanted a few words. I stopped and walked toward a young soldier in uniform. He walked toward me as he sidestepped other people to reach me before we were separated by the crowd. We finally met, and I recognized his face, but I could only remember his first name was John who spoke to me a little out of breath but with rapid-fire words.

"'I want to speak with you . . . let me buy you a cup of coffee!'

"'Okay, John, let's go!'

"I complimented him on his uniform and put my hand on his shoulder guiding him to a nearby coffee shop. Then his surname came to me: Papodakis . . . John Papodakis.

"We entered the small coffee shop and ordered our coffee. John was not interested in small talk but was anxious to say something of importance to me. I waited patiently as he spoke.

"'Teacher, I'm going to make a confession to you. I just came back from the front and saw a lot of death around me. I was in the trenches killing the enemy, and my friends were being killed on either side of me, but . . . do you know what I was thinking?'

"'What, John? Were you thinking of your safety, your family and that you might die at any minute?'

"He spoke as fast as the machine guns he must have faced and I looked at him intently, giving him my fullest attention.

"'No, Teacher, I was thinking of that fifty cent coin that I stole from that girl during our gym recess.'

"'What are you talking about?'

"He had a look of frustration as if he'd been wanting to tell me this for a long time and that I'd surely know just what he was talking about as soon as he started his story. John continued.

"'Do you remember the incident. You did it, didn't you?" he asked, "you were the one that threw the coin, weren't you?'

"I connected with what he was talking about but wanted him to say more, as if more words would make him feel better. It was important to take pressure off him so I replied gently,

"'Oh, John, forget it.'

"'No, Teacher, I can't. My conscience was with me in those trenches.'

"I thought to myself one word, *Amazing!*' This young man was inches away from death in war, and his conscience spoke louder than his personal safety or the likelihood that he was going to die any second. I again tried to comfort him.

"'No, John, you have been through a lot and have grown up to be a good man. Forget about it. You can't worry about it anymore.'

"He didn't let up. His intensity seemed to actually heighten. The thoughts kept in storage for years leaped out hurriedly.

"'I am worried about it, it has always been on my mind; you taught me many lessons in that Greek school; but this was one of the most important, if I can find this girl I want to apologize personally.'

"'John, she's not a girl anymore . . . she's all grown up, married, and has moved away.'

"I didn't know that for sure, but I really wanted him to recover and get on with his life. He'd purged himself of these pent-up emotions and seemed relieved. He shook my hands warmly, and, after trading addresses, we said our good byes.

"I walked home with some powerful thoughts. I'll never forget that young man telling that story on the verge of tears. What a conscience! I had a smile but found myself emotional too. The impact of causing a personality change in a person and having no idea I'd done it was an awakener for me. Many events have happened in my life that are etched in my mind and will last forever. This story of the conscience was one."

Ilse Beckmann, in her story, "The Tapestry Of My Life", relates what life was like for German citizens before, during, and after the war. Her entry will take us a bit out of my year-by-year chronological sequencing of the other stories but I chose to keep her stories together. Germany structured their organizations differently than America and they are worth noting.

Although this book is mostly about America's past I find it critical that we meet people from other countries who immigrated to the United States and the conditions which encouraged their moving to a new land.

1939
War Begins!

"I was in Hamburg living as a nanny when the war broke out. Most of us had no idea what had happened or what would happen. Hitler had invaded Poland.

"Women in Germany, as a general rule, didn't follow politics closely. The men's slogan was 'Politics are dirty!' I never learned, as a young woman, why the invasion took place. There must have been something brewing at the time.

1942
Living With Bombs

"Many times, when I would come home from concerts or whatever outing I attended, I had to return using a commuter train getting off at the last stop where the family lived. There were many times when I was traveling that the American bombers were bombing Hamburg and our trains had to stop as we ran for shelter. Often, it was a long time before they went away and we could continue our trip. They sometimes returned with a new group of planes after they had re-loaded with more bombs. We would have to get off the train again, hide, and get back on when they left.

"One night, when I got off the train after such a trip, I continued on a walkway that I took to get to the house where I was staying. Suddenly, there were planes approaching again and I could hear the anti-aircraft fire from the German guns. Normally, I'd be called to a shelter but I was alone and trying to get home as fast as possible.

"As I was rushing along, something fell from the sky and landed beside me. It was a shell from German guns! It was so scary. This was one of many war experiences.

1943
My Father in War

"My father, at this time, was a car driver and forced to be a Nazi Party member to keep his government job. There were many divisions in the Party and he was in the transportation pool, the least political. All citizens had to help with the defense of the country. Father went away for weeks at a time to help make barriers to stop possible invaders. That was dictated to him and the others at the time. I'm not sure of the details as I was away from home. They also had to dig out trenches along the coastline.

1943
Early War Duty

"At that time, every German girl between the ages of 16 to 19 had to perform some type of war duty. I was sent to be with a farmer's family.

"They called me on the telephone to tell me which farm I was assigned to and where. During the conversation, I had an immediate question, 'Do I have to milk cows?' (I was afraid of doing that.)

'Yes' was their immediate answer.

"Now, that was a concern to me for several reasons. I knew that when winter came, the cows are in the barn for milking. When they start swishing their tail back and forth there was a good chance that I would get a swat across my face with their tails that had earlier been dangling in manure!

"I only had to do six months of such duty because of my home economics training while other girls my age had a full year's obligation.

"Luckily, my military term included summer months. I went out in the field to milk the cows, even in the rain. The cows didn't care if I was uncomfortable or not. They had to give milk, not make me happy! Furthermore, I had the easiest cow to milk which made me grateful. You must remember, I was a city girl, certainly not a farm girl.

Late 1930s & Early 1940s
My Own Pre-School

"In the farming towns, the hired men were all at war and the women were simply too busy to raise their children full time. As a result, they were sent to day care at early ages until age six.

"I had good success because I loved children and did a lot of planning to make sure I gave them the same training they would have received at home.

"I had young girls as helpers who didn't plan on becoming teachers but were satisfied to help.

"It was a long day for these children. It would start early in the morning and lasted until about 5 o'clock in the evening. Most mothers picked their children up at noon, took them home for lunch, then returned them for the afternoon session.

"The last center that I taught at was a large one. There were 80 children under my care. About 20 would stay for lunch and I fixed their lunch. If the weather was nice, we moved outside.

"At the time they also changed our handwriting style from 'Old German' to the letters that we use now. The paperwork was also my job.

"We did gymnastics with rings. Part of my lessons included hygiene. There were wash bowls available for the children to practice such habits as proper brushing of their teeth. I also taught them songs and games.

"When the day care center closed, I walked many of the children back to their homes if their mothers were unable to pick them up.

"At this time, my parents lived in Meldorf which was close to where I worked and lived in Baugen Stadt. I rented a room there just under the attic. There was a very steep ladder up to my room. It was cold during the winter when I returned from work but was heated when the owner of the house below started the iron coal stove.

"About this time, I got very sick. I contracted diphtheria and afterward came down with scarlet fever. I had to be in quarantine for five or six weeks and was only allowed to speak with others through a window.

"But I was not alone in that regard as many Germans died at that time. It was a long, hard battle fought under cold conditions with little food to keep our strength.

1942
Kindergarten Teacher Training

"In 1942, after my six month obligation on the farm and pre-school days, I decided to become a full-fledged kindergarten teacher. At 19, I received training in different government courses.

"The first practical training I had was when I was working for a woman who had already passed her examination. I worked for her in an apprenticeship program. She turned out to be a life-long friend, Bertha Schulz, who died in 1997.

"One year after that, at 20, I passed the examination. At that point, I had my own first day care center assigned to me in a small farm town.

"I was trained and employed by the state to lead my own day care center under government regulations. All employees were forced to say 'Heil Hitler!' like everyone else.

"The war was heating up at that point and it affected my school many times. When air raid warnings came that American bombers were approaching we had to rush down into the cellar to avoid getting hurt by flying debris.

Following is another story from Ilse. This one shows how German POWs were treated.

1944
Somewhere in Eastern Germany

"There was total darkness in that railroad freight car. But there were sounds—moaning sounds of thirty men in pain. And there were smells—smells of human waste from men with no control of their bowels. This waste became the floor covering upon which they slept after a day's work. There was no fresh air coming into the car and no way for the overpowering smells to leave. The men's discomforts were sealed inside each night. These conditions would be etched forever in these men's memories.

"Nobody outside the car was concerned about these conditions until morning. That's when the freight car's large sliding door was opened by the guards. Then, that suffocating smell burst through the door's opening as the men struggled to stand for their next day of hard labor. The guards turned their faces away as the prisoners slowly climbed down from the train. The smell was that bad.

"The men's faces had a temporary look of relief as they left the car each cold morning. Next, they were fed a watery soup to carry out their demanding manual labor. This soup caused diarrhea in most of them which covered the freight car's floor. As they slept, it stuck to their clothes day and night.

"Who were these men and what had they done to deserve such inhumane treatment? They were German soldiers held as prisoners by their Russian captors in the eastern part of Germany. Russia had successfully turned back the German offensive into Russia. They chased the retreating Germans and captured much of what was once German land.

"What was their work? They were forced to rip up the old German railroad tracks and replace them with a different gauge Russian tracks.

"Many of the prisoners were injured changing these rails. Through neglect, their wounds worsened. Some had wounds, serious infections, and open sores making their bones visible. The crust of filth had caked itself on these men and there was no hope of medical help. The Russians certainly weren't interested in anything but their railroad. If a prisoner was considered so sick he couldn't work there were two choices: either kill him or release him knowing he'd never get far in such poor health.

"One prisoner was released with his shin bones clearly exposed below his ragged pants. He walked to his parents' home in Luebek, Germany. In pain, he knocked on the door hoping not to frighten anyone with his appearance. This man was my brother, Walter. My parents barely recognized him.

Ilse continues with post-war commentary.

1945
American Forces in Germany

"The American forces came into Germany only at the end. They took what was left of the German military supplies and many German prisoners, including my husband, Guenther. The people from England came up to Northern Germany and they divided up the areas with the French to stabilize the country.

"We felt a degree of hopelessness. There was simply no involvement in any form of politics on the part of German citizens. I remember seeing the German soldiers being marched, as prisoners, in rows to be placed later in makeshift prisons. If some of the soldiers were unable to walk in formation they were simply shot and left by the side of the road. It was a matter of wondering what would happen next and who would be alive.

"We were unaware of the concentration camps. Hitler could not afford for the German public to know of them because internal forces would rise up to kill him. If everyone in Germany knew that we had the concentration camps there would be a civil war. There were a lot of German citizens who were friendly with Jewish people.

"There was a 'Putsch' which was an uprising of German military officers to kill Hitler. But it was unsuccessful. Those organizing the attack were confident they would be able to kill him but a traitor revealed the plans. Hitler was warned and the rebels were all killed.

"Hitler's secret headquarters were very well hidden in the forest. He was injured during the assassination attempt but that was the extent of it.

"Here in America, many people think the camps were only for Jewish people but that was not true. A lot of anti-Hitler Germans were also imprisoned.

"I often saw some of the SS. They were all tall and healthy men. If a young man was both large and healthy he was forced to join the SS, an elite segment of the military. My mother's cousin's son was very tall with Nordic qualities including blonde hair. He was forced to join and was eventually killed near Latvia in a train wreck. This man was formerly a silversmith and I now have some of his nice jewelry including a ring he made for my confirmation. I often corresponded with his wife.

1945
Bad Times in Germany

"Times were very bad in Germany. No one knew if they would be alive the next day. You couldn't buy anything even though you had money, there were no goods. The all-out bombing of our country put us in a constant state of anxiety.

"Living conditions were desperate and I figured that something was better than nothing. It was simply a matter of no hope for anything better as Germany was losing the war. There was not enough to eat, nothing to buy, and we always heard news of our friends dying in battle. Every day we would hear of someone's son or husband being killed.

1945
War Is Over!

"It finally happened, we lost the war! We all knew it was just a matter of time and hoped the end would bring some form of relief to our lives.

"Foreign soldiers were all over our country. The English soldiers were in North Germany and the Americans were in the south. We were completely occupied by foreign troops. I would see the soldiers marching through the city when I was walking between my in-law's home and the doctor's office. I was reluctant to be out walking near them as we had lost the war and I was alone. It was uncomfortable to live in your home country when foreign troops were everywhere. The war was over in May and I quit my job in June.

My baby was due to be born in September of 1945. In Germany, it was not an ideal time to enter the world."

———————

Following are two stories from a book which I did not write but collaborated on. It was titled "The Captain and The Captives" and written by Andrea Goldthwaite. She did a wonderful job writing this book and certainly deserves a separate reading on its own merit. Andrea shares her WW II stories below:

GOLD STARS FOR EVERYONE
1945

"Every Sunday, and many weekdays, my family visited the Fall River neighborhood's Holy Name Church to pray for the safety of all members of the Armed Forces serving in World War II. I could not help but notice that, as time went by, there were fewer and fewer young men in attendance. I wondered why. When I asked my Mom that question she answered with sadness:

"'They have gone to war, Andrea.'

"On one particular Sunday morning, I noticed that there was a new glass case situated just to the left side of the main altar. After Mass, the family approached the glistening glass case to examine the hundreds of names of young men and women in the war. Without hesitation, my eyes became fixed on three family names: my brother, John, my Uncle Harry, and my godfather, John Murphy. Instantly, I noticed that several of the other names had gold stars next to them. Curiously, I asked my Mom and Dad:

"'What do the gold stars mean?'

"My parents, evidently wanting to spare me any grief, replied in a loving tone:

"'A star means that the person is most important, special, and loved.'

"I was quite saddened by the absence of gold stars near my loved ones' names, as I assumed the absence of gold stars meant that my own family members were not as important or special or loved. I decided that I needed to prove to everyone that my relatives were very loved. Even though I had never personally known any of those sailors who were going to war, I felt a strong desire to help any Armed Force member whom I knew.

Early the next day, I reported to school with one goal in mind: to earn as many gold stars as I could. I was fully prepared to remedy the terrible mistake which someone at the church had made. I worked very hard all week long until the time came for the weekly Friday tests. I aced every test and actually earned FOUR gold stars. At the end of class that cold afternoon, I shivered while walking home by way of the church. Slowly I opened the giant heavy oak doors, and pattered down the church aisle. I paused as I listened to the echo of my steps in the large, silent, and empty church.

"Standing in front of the glass case, I reached into my navy blue uniform pocket and took out three stars, which I had peeled from my award-winning papers. Methodically opening the glass case, my eyes searched for the names of the people whom I loved so very much. I could hear my heart beat as I moistened each star and with great excitement stuck one next to each name of the people I loved: Uncle Harry, by brother John, and my godfather, John Murphy. Looking at the list of names I noticed that Aunt Ann and Aunt Mary's names were missing from the list of important people. I was a bit confused because I knew that, in a way, they had been serving their country when they were captured by the Japanese and put into prison camps. I thought that I would ask my parents about their omissions from the list at a later time. My immediate mission complete, I headed home while jumping in each and every ice speckled puddle along the way, pleased with the thought that everyone at church would see how loved my relatives were!

"With a glint in my eye, I bounded into the kitchen, kissed Mom, and washed up, knowing that I had done a very unselfish and kind deed. Clearly, I remember just bursting with joy. In writing of this account, I realize my readers may not understand why I didn't tell an adult what I had done. The reason for not telling anyone had been part of my early education: when a person did a kindness for another, it was kept a secret. I was taught that the inner feeling of happiness and pride would be sufficient reward. That evening my family and I enjoyed every single morsel of hamburger, mashed potatoes, and green beans on our dinner plates. When dinner was over, my big sister, Debbie, and I were excused from the table to wash the dishes, an evening ritual in the Duffy household.

"We always had such fun doing the dishes. Sometimes we would stop our work, sit on the floor, and with pieces of chalk play tic, tac, toe on the side of the old-fashioned black slate sink. Debbie and I always had so much fun playing 'schoolteacher' while writing on the outside of the sink. The simple fun of playing school, marbles, blocks, and jacks with my sister stands out in my mind as being some of the most happy and carefree times I ever had as a child during my early years."

News From The War

"On such occasions, it took us several hours to finish our assigned task but we always completed our designated job with smiles on our faces. Suddenly, the ringing of our old hand-held phone interrupted the after-meal chatter and clatter. Putting down her cup of steaming tea, my Mom answered it with her normally cheerful:

"'Helloooooo.'

"Suddenly, she was crying uncontrollable while muttering:

"'No, Father Harrington, no, they all are not dead. No! What do you mean? Not one Navy or Army person ever came or called here. NO! You are wrong!'

"Our whole family was immediately devastated! It appeared as though my uncle, brother, and godfather were all dead! How could this be? There was not time to think because within a few minutes the members of the Holy Name Church Women's Guild, whom the priest had already notified, descended upon the Duffy household with cakes, pies, cookies, brownies, and other assorted delicacies. Mrs. Conlin, our next-door neighbor, presented me with a plate of the most delicious-looking chocolate fudge. When this nice next-door lady picked me up and rocked me I felt very grateful for all the food, the likes of which I had never seen. I was thrilled that I did not have to stand in long lines on this day to get the ration of sugar and butter which I knew were in these delivered treats. I stood in those long lines many times and had developed a deep appreciation of the goodie's ingredients.

"I recall being very excited about the evening's commotion. Each and every time the front doorbell rang I ran to the door. Inviting the guests into my home, I saw in front of me an assortment of penguin-looking nuns from the Sacred Heart Order. There they stood dressed in their black and white habits while clutching their long rosary beads. They, along with Father Harrington, had come to pay their respects to all family members and started to pray and sing. As the evening wore on, I was softly lulled to sleep to the words of the melodic song, 'Immaculate Mary our Hearts are on Fire.'

"My red-faced Dad had been just beside himself and looked like he was in a fog. Urgently and without warning, my Dad awakened me with his resounding deep voice:

"'This is ridiculous! We have no official word that anything had happened to any single member of our family. The only official word I have is about my sisters, Sister Ann and Sister Mary, but at least they are alive! Father Harrington, help me make some phone calls. By gosh, my son is supposed to be in ROTC training in Texas!'

"After what seemed like hours, it was discovered that John Duffy was alive and asleep in his barracks at Texas A&M College. Next, a ship-to-shore call was made to Harry's ship in the North Atlantic. Harry was alive and well! In fact, he was thrilled to share news of his responsibilities as Vice Admiral, and was most befuddled by Dad's call. In addition, Lt. John Murphy, was also found alive and well on the coast of Dover, England!

"Yet, the mystery was not yet solved. With a monotone voice, my Dad glared at Father Harrington and shouted:

"'Young man, where in tarnation did you get the idea that my relatives who are protecting our country died? Speak up!'

"With a slight Irish brogue, the priest recounted his visit to the church that afternoon and noticed the new stars near our family's names in the glass case. He had been so surprised to see three more stars that he did not check with the Church Gold Star Committee that always kept everyone informed about tragedies. The entire Duffy household was stone silent. After all, Dad was yelling at a priest!

"Bolting from his position near the food-crowded table, Dad bounded over to me and whispered every so slowly:

"'Andrea, do you know anything about gold stars near the names of your uncle, your brother, and your godfather?'

"Dad truly looked as if he were near the collapse stage; after all, he was emotionally shaken by the serious situation of each of his sisters, the nuns. Now, he thought the rest of his family had died. He raised his voice and continued:

"'Well, do you?'

"Very slowly, rubbing sleep from my eyes, I recounted every single detail of my quest to make the three important people in my life as special and important as they could be. Loving the captive audience, I told of my mission to obtain the gold stars, the walk to church alone, and the happy feeling in my heart as I stuck each gold star next to the name of my three favorite war heroes. The family members, the priest who was now sweating, the neighbors, and the nuns listened to the unraveling tale of the mystery of the gold starts.

"Finally, Mom and Dad told me the real meaning behind a gold star. It signified that the person had died for his or her country. Shocked at this revelation, I jumped up and proclaimed my undying love for these relatives and my sorrow at all the problems I now knew were caused by my good intentions. Like dominoes slowly falling over one by one, the guests began to have tears of joy and smiles of relief that the John Duffy, John Murphy, and Harry Koosel families would still have time to enjoy more days of togetherness. Each of their loved ones was alive and very well, indeed!

The War is Over!

"It was not too long after that emotionally charged night that World War II was over. The heavy black air-raid drapes came off the the windows and family members began returning home. ON a clear and sunny Saturday morning, all members of my family attended the Fall River Victory Parade. There we stood all in a row and watched as the high-stepping and smartly dressed Durfee High School Marching Band played the "Battle Hymn of the Republic" as they paraded down Main street. While listening to that band I decided that I too, would someday join that band and would play a trumpet while wearing the black and red school colors."

"After a few minutes, what seemed like hundreds of ladies, each wearing a large gold star, marched in front of the spectators. Dad slowly lifted me up, held his hand over his heart, and with a tear falling on his cheek, stood at attention. I did not dare to ask where my aunts, the nuns, were at this time, but I knew that our family would not be the same until they both returned home. At long last, I fully understood what a gold star meant. So I help my hand over my chest and quietly cried for all of the Fall River men and women who gave their lives for their United States of America. I wondered if some of those sailors whom we watched sail out to war from the Cape Cod Canal that memorable day, not too long ago, were among those whose deaths we were mourning."

WW II Prisoners of War: Rescue at Los Banos
1946

"I distinctly recall that joyous day in May of 1946, when I finally met my two aunts for the very first time. The air of excitement bounced off the walls as echoes of glee reverberated throughout our home. Dad had received special permission from Mother Superior Mary Joseph of the Maryknoll Motherhouse to have his sisters, the Duffy nuns, nursed back to health by their brother.

Though they had both been in the states for some time, neither was able to travel because of having been so very ill from their mistreatment as Prisoners of War. Dad told us that he was going to get the juiciest meats, the ripest fruits, and the freshest vegetables for his two older sisters. His lips quivered as he said:

"'Andrea, I am going to restore and rebuild their bodies and their spirits.'

Home at Last!

"He was determined. On this day, a car's horn was heard blasting with triumph from the driveway below the dining room windows. As I looked out I saw my Dad's large figure leaping down the stairs and for the first time in 16 long years, flying into the outstretched arms of his two sisters. Even today, so very many years later, the image of their long overdue reunion is still etched in my mind.

"Both of my aunts looked worn, tired, and so pitifully thin; the one from tuberculosis contracted as a prisoner in Korea, the other from years of abuse as a prisoner of the Japanese in a Philippine prison camp. Debbie and I volunteered to give our aunts our bedroom for the next full year while we occupied the narrow and extremely lumpy couch in the living room. During the following few weeks, the sagas of my aunts' captures and internments slowly began to unfold.

"Each evening our entire Duffy family gathered around the dining table and enjoyed the most generous portions of the finest of foods. Dad was keeping his word by providing sumptuous meals not only to his sisters, but also to any person who joined our table. After the war years of meager servings, I certainly appreciated a good meal . . . let me tell you! Following dessert one evening, Aunt Mary was the first to reveal the details of her imprisonment by the Japanese. While looking me squarely in the eye she began:

"'The date was December 8, 1941 when Japanese detectives entered our mission in Shingishu, Korea. Immediately, I knew that was the last day I had built my last happy and carefree tower out of blocks.'

"I shook my head in amazement as I listened to her every word. With a weakened voice, turned to a whisper from tuberculosis, she continued. She recounted that Japanese policemen stormed into the convent, told the sisters war had been declared, and put them under house arrest. From that time on, the sisters survived on the scarce donations of foods from the Korean people. She recounted the story she had written in her debriefing letter for the Maryknoll Archives. It seems as though the residents of the area were very thankful for both the religious and the medical assistance offered at their mission-hospital, and would donate what food they could. With obvious love glowing from her eyes she continued:

"'One lady came from Gishu and hearing that we were short of meat and eggs returned to her home on 'shanks' mare' and came on the next day, carrying a live chicken and a few eggs. She had walked thirty-six miles to bring the food.' (Maryknoll sisters Collections, Maryknoll Mission Archives.)

"She told us that from this one donation the sisters made savory chicken, which fed more than 14 nuns on that same day! Slowly, she continued by telling us that she was the last of ten missionaries to be told to leave Korea. She was forced to board a boat and travel to Japan where she and others were under armed guard 24 hours a day. She mentioned their being allowed to exercise only twice during that time and being forced to have daily roll call once in the morning and once at night. Leaving some extensive gaps in her descriptions, she told of the day the sisters in her group were ushered onto a ship, the *SS Gripsholm*, and set sail for the United States. Based on my subsequent research, it appears that there was an agreement between the United States and Japan for an exchange of prisoners of of war. The nuns from Shingishu appear to have been that part of that exchange.

"When Sister Mary William arrived in the states in the summer of 1942 she was gravely ill with tuberculosis and spent the following three and a half years in a hospital in Monrovia, California. Though I was shocked to have heard about Aunt Mary's experiences with armed guards, guns and roll calls, I would later be even more stunned by Aunt Ann's recounting of her imprisonment. Even now, as I am scribing these words, I find these following memories of my other aunt to be heart-wrenching.

"Dad, seated at the head of the table, poured a glass of wine for each person. Mom had used her very best china, crystal, and linen for these homecoming meals. Immediately, all eyes focused on Aunt Ann as she said:

"'I lift my glass in peace with sincere thanks to God for our rescues.'

"I reached over and held Aunt Ann's wrist. Wow, my seven-year-old thumb and index finger easily went all the way around that wrist. She was so very skinny. Then, very slowly and with carefully enunciated words, Aunt Ann revealed her story of capture, imprisonment, and rescue.

"On December 8, 1941, Sister Annie had been helping some little children there in St. Lucena, the Philippines, learn how to read, write, and sing. She looked at me and said:

"'I was teaching them your favorite song, Andrea Loretta, Immaculate Mary Our Hearts are on Fire.'

"I looked at her through misted eyes and silently thought, *And I was playing with my blocks, Aunt Ann.'* With quivering lips, she continued:

"'Without warning and with guns blazing, the song was interrupted as the Japanese invaded the island and their planes bombarded us with bullets.'

"She described how they all ran and hid under the convent saying:

"'We could hear the ratter-tat-tat as the bullets dropped on our tin roof three and a half stories above us. (Maryknoll Sisters Collection, Maryknoll Mission Archives.)

'I was told that the invading Japanese forces took thousands of people, including men, women, nuns, and priests, as prisoners of war. I looked at her and thought that it must have been horrible to have your individual freedom gone and controlled by someone else. Even at the young age of seven, I could not imagine how she could have coped with that situation. I recall feeling very angry at her captors.

"With goose bumps appearing on her arms, she told how she and the other Maryknoll sisters were marched into a prison camp surrounded by barb wire. Aunt Anne told me:

"'I thought that I was going to die. I was so afraid! It was only my faith that would help me each and every day.'

"She described the contents of her hut: the wooden slab on which she was to sleep for so very many years, the small wooden bowl in which the guards would throw a few spoonfuls of rice and the limited amount of drinking water given to each. On occasion, the sweltering heat would be relieved by rain. During a downpour, Aunt Annie, a natural leader, decided that she would first appoint a lookout, then lean out the window of the hut, and catch water in her empty wooden bowl. This precious necessity of life would be shared with other nuns. If the guards had caught this innovative woman involved in such a simply thing as catching water to drink, every single nun in that hut would have been shot.

"Aunt Annie was a highly intelligent lady who had taught herself to read at an early age. Not only did she have a broad range of knowledge, she also had a great instinct for survival. So, it was not surprising that she developed a scheme that would allow her to endure her suffering. She went on:

"'Within a few weeks of arrival at the camp, I realized that we were all going to die unless we had more food.'

"Suddenly, she stopped and said:

"'Look at my arms, Andrea. Even now, I am shaken with fear with thoughts of my many years as a prisoner of war.'

"While Aunt Ann was scared and full of fear in a land so many miles from home, I, too, had been so afraid, so worried, and so concerned for her and all Americans involved in this war. 'She continued on:

'I approached the guards on duty outside of my hut. I asked them if I could have permission to walk around the inside perimeter of the prison camp and say my prayers to my God.'

'Surprisingly, the Japanese captors granted this request to my Aunt Annie and mentioned that one other nun could accompany her each day.

"Under the blazing Philippine sun my aunt, Sister Annie, would walk several steps, kneel in prayer, rise, walk some more, and repeat her movements. The Japanese never knew that she was doing anything other than praying. Each time she knelt in prayer and reached for her rosary by her side, my aunt picked up various kinds of bugs, insects, and worms that she carefully hid in her long black and gray nun's dress. Occasionally, she would find grains of rice scattered at the edge of the fence. Instinctively, she knew these few grains were from the Catholic Filipino children who sneaked under the cover of darkness to deposit a bit of their own food for the Sisters, some of whom had been their friends.

"Each time she returned to her hut, the companion nun secretly brought in two medium-sized stones which were blistering hot from having been in the hundred and twenty-degree sun. Diligently, Aunt Annie placed her catch of the day between these rocks, pulverized this source of protein, and from the heat of the stones cooked the morsels into a tasty and palatable treat. Always, my aunt shared these delicacies with the other Sisters in her hut.

"In paying my Aunt Ann a tribute, Mother Mary Joseph wrote in the Maryknoll Archives, "' . . . her managerial skills and culinary gifts were put to the test. She devised a simple fireless cooker which provided the necessary energy to bake the beans (meaning the rice and bugs) long after the meager . . . food supply had given out for the day."'

"She continued to relate her memories even though they were obviously so painful. She said that on the evening of February 22, 1945, she and her fellow prisoners were sharing their meager morsels of rice, laced with the bug catch-of-the-day, when planes were heard overhead. In the dimness, they saw the insignia of the American planes and instinctively knew that their prayers over the years were being answered. Through the blackened sky, she saw the mountain sides "glow on fire" as the surrounding Japanese-held hills were bombarded. During the hour's air raid, the Filipino guerrillas crept to within yards of their camp where they hid in the darkened shadows until morning. She later would write: ' . . . we were anxious that the time of liberation was near.' (Maryknoll Sisters Collection, Maryknoll Mission Archives.)

"On this warm night in 1946, my Dad was so totally overcome with this true story that he rose from his chair and embraced his sister, Ann. My aunt placed her glass of wine on the table, looked straight at my Dad who was wiping a tear from his eye and tried to console him:

"'Dear brother, your prayers helped us to be rescued from the Los Banos prison camp.'

"She then motioned for her younger brother, my Dad, to sit next to her and after brushing a tear from her own cheek, and, with great effort, continued her story. She said that the following morning, February 23, 1945, all prisoners were gathered on the dirt-covered yard as daily morning roll call started. Each sister was answering to her own name when from the sky above was heard the loud hum of hundreds of American planes. She looked at me and painted me an image:

"'Andrea, my heart was awakened when I saw the planes of my country dropping over two hundred paratroopers from the sky. They looked like angels floating from the heavens above.' (Maryknoll Sisters Collection, Maryknoll Mission Archives."

"Even today I am still shaken by her vivid description of that moment of hope. Those angels were the brave American men of the 11th Airborne Division. Each member of the family was on the edge of our emotions as she continued. She looked at Debbie and in a tone barely audible continued her story:

'The guerrilla ground troops hidden away during the night charged the camp with such great force they killed every Japanese guard and did not seriously hurt any of the pitiful prisoners.' (Maryknoll Sisters Collection, Maryknoll Mission Archives."

"After the camp was secured, the young, strong, Filipino and American men helped my Aunt Ann and the survivors. Shortly, they discovered that each prisoner was in such a weakened condition that not one could even carry the smallest of bags.

"They groaned as they walked a half a mile then boarded a tank that rolled onto a ship. It crossed Laguna de Bay while under Japanese fire. The worn, exhausted, and joyful prisoners arrived at the secured

American occupied section of Manila, Philippines. At this point in the discussion my Aunt Ann broke into sobs as she said:

'What a wonderful sight to see Our Stars and Stripes flying as we rode up the hill.' (Maryknoll Sisters Collection, Maryknoll Mission Archives.)

"What she had written in her debriefing at Maryknoll, I think, sums up her innermost thoughts of that Day of Rescue by the 11th Airborne Division at Los Banos. She wrote:

'It was a tense moment for all as Our Grand Flag waved its welcome after three years!" (Maryknoll Sisters Collection, Maryknoll Mission Archives.)

"I was told that at the conclusion of WW II, the only long-term prisoners of war to have survived their captivities at the Los Banos prison camp were those Maryknoll nuns in my aunt's hut, undoubtedly in large part due to my Aunt Ann's efforts. In recounting that wonderful day of rescue she looked around the table at her openly crying members and in a still shaky voice said,

'The Japanese captors took away my spirit, my heart, and my freedom. They could never take away my determination, my faith in my God, my love for my country, or my soul.'"

What a wonderful tribute to those nuns along with the religious freedom they so revered as developed by their Catholic church training. Again, I give thanks to both Andrea and the Maryknoll Mission Archives for sharing their stories. Andrea's book is certainly worth its own separate reading to gain an even deeper understanding of the families left behind while our soldiers fought in two major wars.

Mr. Bill Hall and I wrote a book describing the life of his wife Joanne shortly after her death. The book, titled "Celebrating The Life Of Joanne Finnegan Hall", contains a post-war passage relating her perspective following WW II. He related the story to me and our words are below:

Post-War Thoughts
1946

"One of the good things about Pop and Emma Finnegan was that they always sat their children down each evening around the kitchen table to do their homework. They would all help each other and were overseen by their parents. Pop Finnegan stressed learning to his family and was often heard to make the following statement:

"'An educated man was one who read the paper each day from beginning to end.' "It seemed that this educational focus helped develop each of the Finnegan children's significant potential. There were many spirited conversations about politics. As a result, Joanne was always an ardent patriot for the United States, especially for FDR. All her life, she closely followed the political scene.

"Following is clear evidence of her independent thinking and how it translated into her talented writing skills. She was always so caring for others less fortunate while being grateful for what she had herself. This Christmas letter was written by a sixteen-year-old Joanne Finnegan:

"EIGHTEEN SHOPPING DAYS 'TILL CHRISTMAS"

"Here in exactly five words, you have said, sadly enough, just what Christmas means to us now.

"This year is our first peaceful Christmas in four years. That is, it is peaceful for us. Taking advantage of this fact, we are all planning our extra-special Christmas. However, let us remember the children in Europe and Asia. While we are having all our beautiful presents, some Dutch girl or boy will be having one of those Red Cross boxes to which we gave our castaways while we are eating Christmas dinner, a German girl may be getting a handout from an American Army camp.

"Christmas has degenerated in meaning from the day of rejoicing over the birth of Christ to the day of foolish pleasure that it is now. Let us take it back to its original status.

"The one way that we can make Christmas what it should be is to help bring complete peace to the world. We must have a world where never again will there be empty chairs at the Christmas dinner or any little children whose fathers have been killed to save us. We must forget our prejudices and think only of the good in everyone.

"We must cooperate to the fullest extent to make our various peace organizations successful. Perhaps if we individually do our best to make everyone, everywhere happy and materially secure, some day, in the not-too-distant future we shall truly have 'Peace on earth, good will toward men.'"

Joanne Finnegan '46

"That was Joanne Finnegan speaking to us from 1945. I always liked her timeless messages which still make sense. She always had strong feelings about the world and how it was going. Joanne viewed common worldly events without being critical or over-bearing. She also wrote the following essay during her senior year at the Tisbury School:

FREEDOM FROM FEAR

'One of the principle aims of the Atlantic Charter is to ensure the four freedoms to everyone all over the world. At the time this great document was written, we were living under the dread fear that we would be drawn into the European War.

We finally were, and after three-and-one-half years of fighting, on V-E Day everyone looked forward to at least two more years of war in the Pacific. However, in August, 1945, only two months, instead of two years after V-E Day, came the astounding news that Japan had unconditionally surrendered. Since then, the atomic bomb, the weapon that had made possible this wonderful news, has proven to be one of the biggest, if not the biggest, problem faced by the people of the world.

It is the opinion of many intelligent people that the only good done by the bomb was to hasten the defeat of Japan. On the other hand, few people realize that in addition to its destructive power, it might be used constructively in the treatment of cancer and other uncontrolled diseases.

First, let us look at the recently developed atomic principle from the standpoint of its destructiveness. For some time after the bombings of Hiroshima and Nagasaki, nothing definite was heard about the bomb. There were many wild rumors, but the first concrete report was made to Congress this spring by the Lilenthal Committee, composed of the leading men of science and business in the United States. This report gave Congress the frightening news that the bomb could not possibly be kept secret, and there is no scientific defense, as far as we know, for there is no barrier, which can prevent a plane from getting into a country.

Ordinary bombs do damage in a relatively small area, but in an atomic explosion, tens of thousands may die. In the very center, there are no wounded, not even bodies, for people and buildings are all pulverized.

Dr. Harold C. Urey, one of the atomic scientists says, "I am a frightened man. As a scientist, I tell you, there must never be another war. Other issues must wait. Other problems will stand delay. But the main race between mans' powers for evil and his powers for good—that race is close to a decision. The bomb is fused. The time is short. We must think fast and straight." When we hear things like this, how can we help but be frightened? Can there be freedom from fear, when we might be bombed out of existence at any time?

In contrast to this, let us look at one of the constructive uses of the atomic principle. The cause of the second highest death rate for people thirty-five and over is cancer. Last year alone, in the United States, 175,000 Americans died of this disease.

Cancer is a malignant growth, which starts in the body as a result of certain, not yet understood changes in the blood cells. At the close of the war, the campaign against cancer was again started.

Medical researchers have taken great steps forward in their knowledge of this disease. Before a cancer has had time to spread, it can be controlled either by surgery or by X-rays or by radiations. This last method is where the atomic principle comes in because great quantities of artificial radioactivity can be made in the same atomic pile which produces plutonium for the atomic bomb. This plutonium, however, cannot be obtained except by a very expensive process.

Just think of all the money that was spent on the war, and which is still being spent on the atomic tests, to find the destructive power of the bomb! Imagine all the good this money could do, if it were used in medical research—training doctors and scientists and furthering the constructive use of this great power!

When this great power is further developed and used only for the advancement of mankind, we will have eliminated one of the major stumbling blocks to permanent peace. We will also have taken one step further toward complete freedom from fear.

And now, may I close with a quotation from one of Henry Wadsworth Longfellow's famous poems titled:

The Arsenal

*" Were half the power that fills the world with terror,
Were half the wealth bestowed on camps and courts,
Given to redeem the human mind from error,
There were no need for arsenals and forts."*

Despite the war stopping it didn't suggest suffering had come to an end. Other countries were still suffering, further defining the concept of a "World War." Americans who had immigrated to the U. S, decades earlier still felt an allegiance to their mother country and did what the could to help. This segment in Mr. Athanas' life story took place in 1946, over twenty years after he had left his island home as he described in his book "The Life of Emanuel S. Athanas" He shares a story of his paying back what Greece did for him:

1946
Greece

"I felt a need to re-connect with my homeland. This was a problem, as the Germans, in their quest for world domination, had landed on the Dodecanesean Islands. But as the war continued, the British had fought them, forcing their retreat. The British then occupied the islands but had no regard for the Greeks. Many Greeks were starving because the war had left many people without work and without food. Conditions were certainly dismal. Something had to be done, and I felt a responsibility to serve my country.

"Three of us, including my brother, decided to form the "Dodecanesean Transportation Company", and I became its president. Taking the initiative, we appealed to all of the former Dodecanesian citizens living in America to donate food, clothing, money, agricultural implements and other necessities. I promised we would bring the goods directly to the island of Rhodes and the other islands. I directed the donation process here in America, a process taking several months, and began planning for the long and dangerous trip. We felt detached from our native land for too long.

"We chartered an old 10,000 ton cargo ship and loaded it with all the donated supplies. The boat we had to use was so old it couldn't be used in any way for the war. This was an exciting time for us here in America knowing that in spite of war, we could still help our countrymen. We had sampled the good life here in the United States and were only too willing to share in some small way with our old friends and relatives back in the Dodecanese Islands. In May, 1946, all preparations had been made, and we left New York City for Rhodes.

"To travel safely during this courageous thirty-eight day trip required great care. The Atlantic Ocean, during wartime, had many enemy boats, submarines and floating mines ready to inflict damage on unwary travelers. These dangers, to worsen the problem, were randomly scattered making safe navigation an unsure thing. Our old ship could travel at only six miles per hour. The potential danger, however, was offset by the confidence we all shared knowing that we were doing a good thing. Realizing that we would eventually step foot on the same island soil of our birthplaces while surrounded by our relatives and old friends was a compelling reason to push on regardless of the dangers.

"As we neared Lisbon, Portugal we took a major loss in that our propeller came loose and fell into the ocean. We had on board a reserve propeller but lacked the knowledge and tools to put it in place. To be powerless in the ocean is an open invitation to tragedy, and we knew it. The onshore wind and resulting waves could drive us toward the Azores and a possible grounding. We didn't despair. We felt confident that a trip planned for the benefit of so many people couldn't go wrong. Luckily, we were able to use our radio to contact another ship. They came to our rescue and helped install our spare propeller. Those of us on board were so driven, so passionately involved, that the trip was bound to be a success.

"We arrived at Lisbon and stayed for only a few days to resupply our boat. From there we continued on to Pyrees, Greece, as a final restocking site before our ultimate destination of Rhodes.

"On July 10, 1944, we reached the city of Rhodes. Its harbor was such a welcome sight. When we got our first distant glimpse of the city, it was a little confusing. Why were thousands of cheering people lining the waterfront? We suddenly realized they were waiting for us! I will never forget my feeling at that moment. Anxiety was clearly etched on their haggard faces . . . relief was here from the Americanized Rhodians who had not forgotten their countrymen in their time of trouble. We sensed their appreciation and joy filled our hearts.

"We landed amidst the joyful welcome and couldn't help but be startled by the condition of the city and its citizens. Things look so different during and after a war. We didn't expect it to be that bad. Trying not to show our distress, we set about our task of unloading the gifts and supplies into a warehouse that had been assigned us.

"Seeing the many old faces and trying to recognize them as we were working was a challenge. Some brought back memories, but they looked so gaunt any positive identification was difficult. I saw a very tall, old man with gray hair who seemed slightly familiar. *Was it his walk? The way he carried himself? His face without the wrinkles?* I fought to remember.

"He approached me walking in torn shoes revealing dirty socks and wearing a torn, but patched, overcoat. As he got nearer, I recognized those eyes, eyes that spoke of a once strong, disciplined man of authority. It was confirmed when he asked me a question.

'Are you Mr. Athanas?'

"Yes," I answered.

"We each seemed to be remembering our last contact, and it was an impressionable one. It was my old high school principal! The same one who'd given me the slap twenty-one years earlier when I asked if our senior high school class could study for our final exams rather than attend a school picnic! Forgetting the past and cherishing that special moment, we embraced tightly while sharing a few gentle slaps on the back.

"He came to the harbor for help but also because he may have heard that it was I, his former student, who had spearheaded this drive to bring supplies from America to his impoverished Rhodes.

"He spoke with emotion, 'I understand that you brought a ship from America with food and supplies. I am in need. I am poor.'

"I smiled and took immediate action asking my brother, who was managing the warehouse, to stop and help.

"Give this man two large bags of flour. Also give him cloth that he can use for making clothes, some leather, a pair of shoes, and a big bag of rice!"

"As my brother was filling my requests, my principal spoke to me in a quiet and humble voice, 'I'm sorry for the slap.'

"I answered, 'No, don't be sorry. That slap helped me . . . it steeled my character. It made me always respect my superiors. It taught me to be courteous to others. You helped me become a better man.'

"He stood there for a moment taking in what I had said while absorbing the idea he had made a difference in a student's life. For sure, he experienced a nice feeling. On the other hand, the present had to be dealt with too. He needed more help.

'Mr. Athansiadeas, you have given me all these supplies, but I do not know how to take them home. My home is ten miles from here.'

"I answered confidently, 'Don't worry about it.'

"We were using a horse and small wagon to move supplies from the ship to the warehouse. I decided to put it to better use helping out my former principal, so we loaded the wagon with his goods. I remember it was hard work. Each bag we lifted up to the wagon weighed between thirty and forty pounds. We paid a driver to take the wagon and the thankful man home.

"As he pulled himself up on the seat beside the driver I saw something I'll never forget. My old principal was crying but trying a little not to show it. He was so happy and grateful for all that had happened to him. He spoke to me while still trying to preserve his dignity, 'These are tears of joy, don't worry about it. Thank you so much!'

"I realized I'd probably never see him again and had a full appreciation of that wonderful moment. That principal taught me a good lesson. I never held his painful slap to my face against him. I smiled, looked him in the eye, and spoke two heart-felt words I wanted us both to remember,

"'You're welcome.'"

It is heart-warming to read that so many American immigrants, although loving their adopted country, remember their roots and repay when they can.

When the war ended, I found it interesting to interview veterans' individual perspectives on when the war ended. Bob Morgan, in his book "The Life Story of Robert Morgan" said the following:

1945
End of The War

"Where was I when the Germans surrendered? At the time, I was involved in the European theater and stationed in Santa Maria Island in the Azores. I had been there for about a year and was also stationed in Stephenville, Newfoundland.

When I heard that the war was over, within five minutes, I sent home from the Azores a telegram with the following message:

'I just heard the official announcement that the Japanese have signed peace terms that were compiled at Potsdam. Isn't it marvelous and so hard to believe after all these years of bloodshed and bereavements? It sure is lonely now, just sitting here thinking that all the lucky people in the states can celebrate and make merry but I'm still here praying to God that He will let me return soon.'

Larry Dillard in his story, "Memories From The Life Of Larry Dillard", relates his experience with the announcement of the war's ending,

1945
New York City

"On July 25, 1945, after completing all the paperwork, they shipped me and five other Oklahoma guys on a train to New York City. As we got off the train at Grand Central Station, some men met us and we were escorted to the subway which took us to the Manhattan Beach Training Center in Brooklyn.

"There, we started boot camp but it was short-lived. About three weeks later, our country dropped the atomic bomb on Hiroshima, one of Japan's major cities.

"On the night Japan surrendered, I stayed on base. There was a massive celebration that night in Times Square, but I wasn't part of it. Along with quite a few other guys, I was jubilant it was over but not to the point that I wanted liberty. There were enough of my friends around that night and, having heard of Times Square's congestion, I decided to stay put on base.

"No doubt, it was an awesome night in American history. I recall President Truman as he broadcast on radio:

"'Today, we dropped the atomic bomb on Hiroshima!'

"Of course, we had no idea what an "atomic bomb" was. Furthermore, a few days later, a second bomb was dropped on Nagasaki. Didn't Japan believe us the first time? What a period of history! I remember thinking what's this war coming to? A bomb was capable of killing 100,000 people at a time . . . one bomb! Wow!

Ilse Beckmann adds to Germany's post war misery from her book, "The Tapestry of My Life." It was a Post-war German Headline which was reprinted.

1947

---

130 Grams of Fat . . . Per Month!

"A few briquets in the (high pressure) furnace cardboard (in front of) for the shattered windows, a homemade (sewn) skirt made from swiped American parachutes—that was Christmas good luck (fortune, prosperity) for the Germans in the years after the war. On the ration cards in the winter of 1947 for a whole month: a liter of skim milk, 130 grams of lard, 62.5 grams of cheese or curds, 400 grams of meat, 1 lb. sugar or marmalade, 1 lb. fish, 8 kilos of bread, 1.25 kilos nutrients, 8 kilos of potatoes, 20 cigarettes for men and 10 cigarettes for women were allowed. And the distant prospects were bleak. The politicians announced" "An increase of rations to 1800 calories a day is also unlikely in 1948."

"'This provides an idea of what life was like and it was even more difficult when trying to feed a family. As I said earlier, it was not an ideal time for a child to enter the world.'"

Jinny Davis ("Virginia's Voyages") speaks of her days in Washington, D.C. and her connection with the Truman family.

1948
Margaret Truman

"Many of the our government's officials had their daughters enroll at G.W. We had a new sorority established with our own building. One of these young women was Margaret Truman. She and I used to spend much of our free time between classes back at the sorority apartment building.

Our sorority was Pi Beta Phi. I got to know her as she was in several of my classes.

"Margaret's family was highly involved in her education with a tremendous focus on their very bright, mature, yet unpretentious, daughter. Her mother was very "motherly" in her affection for her daughter whom they adored.

"I enjoyed a real advantage when I bought several used textbooks which were once hers. An exceptionally bright student, she had both underlined critical passages and written notes on the pages' margins. I found her comments to be very insightful.

"She often went to school with either her father driving or two Secret Service men. We lived near each other so I would sometimes ride with her when her father was driving. In those days, it was not unusual to see the president in such everyday settings.

"Margaret continued to be a person of interest to me. She was quite naive about things and didn't grasp the intent when certain people "took her up." Once absorbed into their lives it was a major honor to get a celebrity like the president's daughter to attend their various parties. When invited to parties or big social events, she always seemed to be "girlish" but nevertheless excited about being such a "focus" for many people. The fact remains she was from a very small town in Independence, Missouri, which was always known for its hometown atmosphere so typical of small cities.

"It was a wonderful time to be in Washington although wartime made GW virtually an all female institution. The city was filled with all kinds of foreign diplomats, political figures and high-ranking soldiers. Of course, many of these people had daughters, many of which were GW students. But there were also many gorgeous young men in dashing uniforms who loved to dance. I still enjoyed those dances and seemed to have more ball gowns than I had dresses. It was wonderful to see Chief Justice Stone after dinner who often sat in a nearby hotel lounge in a large chair by the fireplace. It was such a casual atmosphere as he "visited" with whoever was there.

———————————

Jinny Davis, (Virginia's Voyages) describes below an interesting job interview in the mid 1940s. Names involved and the magazine's title have been omitted. I include this short story to show what was and what now is:

June, 1946
College Graduation

"Following my graduation from GW in June of 1946, I got a job in a very fancy department store in the city where all the debutantes bought their dresses. My job was in the children's section.

"I planned to move to New England where I had friends but first wanted to land my 'dream job' in Philadelphia. My perfect job was going to be with a famous national magazine dealing with scenery and stories from countries all over the world. Surely, my international exposure and lifelong interest in reading that same magazine would ensure a good fit for both parties. Another argument in favor of my landing that position was the fact that the head of the magazine had been a classmate of my father's in the Naval Academy.

"Believing that one should dress appropriately for a job interview, I selected my finest outfit and traveled to Philadelphia for my interview. While speaking with the female interviewer, I wove into the conversation my many qualifications including my English major college background coupled with my extensive international travel. I added that I had visited many of the same locations featured in their magazine. Asking all of the proper questions to impress during a job interview, I felt confident I'd be looked upon favorably. My background was not in question; but my appearance was. The interviewer shocked me when she declared:

'We don't hire attractive young women. Our experience has been that it takes two years of training to make one useful and by that time such young women usually get married!'

"True, getting married was what many young women did in those days as they weren't encouraged to enter professional careers. College was followed by marriage. Still surprised and disappointed, I answered:

'Well, I'm not going to get married. There's no one I'm interested in. This work is what I want to do!'

"With no apology, she emphasized: 'Well, this is just our policy.'

"I couldn't believe my ears. This was before the days when discrimination practices came under constant scrutiny. I didn't have the nerve to further advance my cause.

"Meekly, I left."

Jinny Davis, in her book "Virginia's Voyages," relates to us below an interesting post-war connection.

1948
I Knew Truman

"President Truman, a wholesome middle westerner, came from a simple background yet evolved into a bright, thoughtful, and respected high achiever. He saw the world through clear, untarnished, eyes. Undoubtedly, those same eyes honed his world view with a penchant for reading before, during, and after his presidential term.

"My knowing him personally, however, helped me rank him high among my favorite presidents. How can one not be impressed by the most powerful man in the world? Observing firsthand his family interaction with Margaret gave me a glimpse of him as a father. Reading, or listening to him on the radio, was one thing, but speaking with him made it personal. As the three of us rode to school, I loved the way he talked. Similarly, when Mrs. Truman spoke at her daughter's college events, we students listened with reverence. Both Truman parents were very much like everyday, conventional, parents.

"We all enjoy the connection with such ordinary people. It is comforting to know we are all more alike than different. An example of this comfort is when a newly installed President Truman met the press for the first time. When the first addressed him as 'Mr. President,' his initial response was: 'Boys, I wish you didn't have to call me that.' I can just hear him saying that based on our brief, and simple, conversations.

"'Unassuming'" is a word that described him best. Because of my special connection with his daughter, I paid special attention when she began her career as a concert singer. Following an unflattering review of her performance in the *Washington Post*, her protective father wrote the critic a blunt, bitter letter later made public.

"As I thought back on our shared rides to George Washington University, and viewed their close relationship, I was not surprised he would protect his daughter whenever she received harsh criticism. He and his wife were just so proud of their daughter. With my close-up, firsthand view of the family's dynamics, I can testify to the purported Truman loyalty.

––––––––––––––––

Jinny Davis, in "Virginia's Voyages", relates below how it felt to lose America's only president who was elected to four consecutive terms.

1946
Where Was I When FDR Died?

"I was in Washington at the time. But before that, not long before he died, he had just voted as I was stood on a street corner as I waited for my next class. I looked up to see him being driven past me in his open Landeau car with its special style roof. What a treat to see him with his traditional cigarette holder on full display.

"Several days later, I was in class with others and we heard a lot of noise outside in the street. We were curious to see what it was all about but we had one of these stinker professors who wouldn't let us go to the windows as he suggested, "It's not our business." He had no idea what was going on so we sat through it all. But the noise from the streets got louder. Finally, we got out of class, merged into the crowded streets, and quickly learned FDR had died.

"That night many people stayed up all night and roamed, as if in a trance, around D. C. It was a terrible shock to the nation. although we were not surprised considering his age and health. Along with him passing by me on the street corner several days before, I had seen him on a number of occasions in connection with my father. We watched him, and other government officials, along city parade routes in this long ago era of innocence. Then, people were not deeply concerned about attacks or assassinations.

'As you know I was a little girl, about seven, when he started serving as our president and was virtually all I knew. He was a good leader, a classically powerful man, most graceful, and never arrogant.'

Jinny Davis, in her story "Virginia's Voyages", describes her take on the end of WW II:

1945
America's Grandest Moment

"I would say America's greatest moment in my lifetime was the ending of World War II. The end of the war was like the sun started shining all day and night. Everybody came home, but many were wounded. It was a period of both extreme joy and heavy sorrow because many didn't return home.

"One of our close friends, a physician, was on a battleship which was sunk as he operated on a patient. The boy on the operating table was on his back and strapped to the table. The enemy fire penetrated the ship's hull and killed the staff along with our doctor friend. The victim, still strapped to the table, was one of the few survivors. All of my father's friends had stories to tell.

"As a little girl, I recall one of his navy friends who had a stare and seemed so withdrawn. I remember his eyes looked vacant, or empty, and always very sad. Those eyes made an impression on me, and not a good one. He was so passive and quiet around us. My memory had nothing to do with reality but just a feeling I pondered as I grew up. The sad eyes told me a story and I finally decided what was wrong: he must have seen something very bad happen and that he might have not done something to fix the situation. He felt there was something he thought he could have done and was haunted the rest of his life with that memory. I've lived with those eyes, and that thought, ever since.

"Yes, the war's end was one of America's grandest moments, but it also brought home some of America's saddest stories."

Jinny Davis, (Virginia's Voyages) describes how Americans in the 1940s and 1950s learned of world happenings:

1940s & 1950s
Keeping Up With World Events

"Keeping up with the world's events back in the 40's and 50's was just so different than today. We listened to the radio every night. Edward R. Murrow was our connection to the world. In fact, radio was the lifeline for Americans during the 1940's. It brought us not only news from Edward R. Murrow but also music and entertainment of all types.

"Radio brought us mystery shows, soap operas, quiz shows, children's hours, great drama and sports. The other thing that was interesting in the early years of the war was the introduction of military news clips which preceded, like today's "Coming Attractions," the feature presentation. Of course, they were in black and white complete with captions and voice overs, but nonetheless, very informative.

"Soon television arrived in many homes. At the end of the war, there were only about 5,000 sets but within six years there were 17 million in America's homes. Television has since made the difference in that we can see events live as they happen."

———————

Joe Didato, in his life story titled "First Generation . . . An Immigrant's Son" told a story about an event in his life which changed his attitude forever. Although it has little to do with American history, the story helps promote gratitude and being an American always seems to help. It occurred while he was preparing to be released from his military stint.

December 15, 1960
Kentucky

"If my memory serves me right, I believe schools had to hold your teaching position if you joined the military. It was nice looking forward to teaching again. January 1, 1961, was my target date when I was to be discharged. But the military decided to release us early for Christmas on Dec. 15, 1960. We were all excited and thankful to be going home early.

"Now, Kentucky may be in the south but I want to tell you it was some cold that day as we waited in formation. We were to get paid first, then dismissed. The different companies got paid but my company waited extra long waiting for our severance checks. Eventually, an officer approached us and announced they couldn't find our checks. Hopefully, they'd have them the next day. Now, you want to talk about a couple of hundred guys doing some serious bitching. We had to wait another day! At that point, one day seemed like a month. I soon admitted it was beyond my control and resigned myself to another night in Kentucky.

"Sure enough, we got paid the next day and said our 'Goodbyes.' I bought a paper to read on the plane. The headlines jumped out at me and I read the full article once I got on the plane.

———————

'AIRLINERS COLLIDE OVER NYC, 127 KILLED!"

'Two airliners flying in fog and sleet collided over New York City, killing 127 passengers and crew members. Another five persons were killed when one of the airliners crashed in Brooklyn, setting off a seven-alarm fire.

The collision occurred between a United Airlines jetliner with 77 passengers and a crew of seven flying from Chicago and a Trans World Airlines Lockheed Super-Constellation with 39 passengers and five crew members arriving from Columbus, Ohio.

The only survivor was an 11-year old boy on the United jet who was thrown clear of the wreck and landed in a snowbank.

The United jet crashed in the crowded Park Slope section of Brooklyn, demolishing a church. Fuel from its tanks ignited to set the neighborhood ablaze. The TWA jet crashed 11 miles to the southeast, on Staten Island. It missed several houses by a few hundred feet.'

"I was positive that the plane in the article was the same plane I was scheduled to be on!" I thought again: *"If the Army hadn't screwed up my pay yesterday, I'd be dead now!* Fate played a big part here. I'm a lucky guy . . . no more bitching."

Chapter 4

The 2000s

This entry is from my life story "Hey, Jay! What's The Story?" It was not an easy one to write but it was an honor to do. The subject of the story is family.

September 11, 2001
New York City

Another Day Of Infamy

"It was my first day of retirement from my teaching career. If I were still teaching on that day, I would be instructing my first period class as I welcomed my new students to the first day of school for that year. For me, however, it was just a day of driving around with my radio on at about 8:45 a.m.

"A bulletin came on my car's radio with a slight sense of of urgency but sounded somewhat softened at first. They said 'At 8:46 a.m., plane had just hit the World Trade Center's North Tower in New York City!' I had no idea what that meant personally except I knew that Pete Ganci, my wife's first cousin and our son Scott's godfather. He was the Chief of the Fire Department of New York. I knew he would be deeply involved.

"I drove home immediately to catch all the details of what had happened on television as I recalled a previous 'big' day in American history—November 22, 1963. On that day of President Kennedy's assassination, I remember listening to the radio in New Hampshire and they kept referring to ' . . . shots fired from a grassy knoll.' The details of that portion of the broadcast were somehow lost during the transmission. I certainly didn't want the same thing to happen on this potentially big news day. It was, indeed, a terrifying day for our country. I needed first-hand viewing.

"When I got home, I hustled to the television and put it on right away. The cameras were rolling to catch all that was happening when, unbeknownst to them, they showed the second attack on the other Trade Tower as it was broadcasted live to a nation of stunned Americans. It was at 9:03 a.m. Both the North and South towers were on fire from those planes smashing them.

"I remember seeing many individuals on top of both buildings and frantically waving out of the windows. The potential victims were told, by way of cell phones, that helicopters would be dispatched soon to pluck them from the building's roof. It wasn't meant to be as it was too hot for any such heroic acts the city's finest were famous for. Would-be rescuers were powerless.

"At the same time, Pete, while directing all of the rescue efforts of the NYFD, was himself directing rescue efforts of evacuating thousands of people in the first, or North Tower.

"In the book 'Chief,' written by Pete's son, Chris, he described what Dan Nigro, fellow firefighter, said of Pete. He said that 'Pete had a look of hatred of the fire, a look he always had when fighting any inferno.' On that day, Dan said Pete had a look on his face which showed his ultimate hatred of any fire he had ever fought.

"The first tower partially collapsed and Pete was nearly buried. In time, he and his surrounding firefighters were able to dig themselves out. He was directing further efforts while on the fly and helped get people out of the area before the rest of the building fell. He was seen picking up fellow firefighters and pushing them away toward safety. He had ordered a new command post to be established north of the tower where they would be safe. The last people that saw him alive figured he was also on his way out they looked back and saw him heading back toward the teetering South Tower screaming, 'there were more men in there to be gotten out!'

"At 10:05 a.m., just an hour after I reached our house and television, I watched the South Tower completely collapse. Little did I realize that Peter was under that collapse. Considering the conditions, his body was retrieved quickly his fellow firefighters.

"We got the call that night from family that Pete had perished. It was a sad night for all of America but especially hard for our family members as we also lost a second family member, Terry Gazzani, who had worked for Kantor Firzgerald, one of the firms losing the most people in the attack. Two family members: gone.

"Family arrangements were made for Pete and Terry. Pete's wake was set for September 14, 2001, just three days after their leaving us. We drove down and continued past the still-smoking city and saw the smoke billowing from the ruins. I remember rolling the window down in our car and smelling the smoke as we passed even miles from the city.

"We attended the wake at the local fire station in Farmingdale where Pete began his career as a volunteer fireman. We were so shocked at the number of firefighters from all over New England and New York who came to pay their respects. There had to have been 15,000 who passed by his casket. I was struck by the brotherhood of it all and so many caring Americans.

"Other outstanding memories followed after we left the funeral services at St. Killian's where Mayor Guiliani spoke glowingly of Pete. I remember his saying, 'Pete chose to go back in.' The last words he said to Pete on the street as the carnage unfolded all around them was, 'Pete, God bless you!'

"As the church service finished, the funeral procession drove through Pete's old neighborhood and the people on the sidewalks were waving their flags as we all drove by. Little kids were saluting to bring even more tears to our eyes. That had come out of their homes knowing the procession would be driving by.

"On a major highway, a man and his young son, who were driving in the opposite direction, facing us, on the Southern State Parkway. Seeing our motorcade, they immediately parked their car on the side of the road, emerged from the car, and saluted as we passed by. It was moving.

"I remember another man who was evidently leaving the scene in the city. Recognizing Peter's motorcade, he jumped out of his car while covered with white soot, and saluted Peter. There was no more holding back the tears; uncontrollable.

"The second memory I will have forever was the extension adders of two firer trucks which formed a 100 foot arch as our funeral procession passed under under them as the American flag was flying from each ladder.

"Following the service at the cemetery, he got his well-deserved 21-gun salute along with high piles of red carnations placed on his casket.

"Upon reflection, I remembered that I once posed a question to Pete asking him what his job consisted of. Being a writer, I commonly ask that question of my clients. He told me stories of having to extinguish fires which had been purposely set in the city as the neighborhood 'citizens' threw rocks and bricks at the firefighters. He summed up his job description with,

"'I'm just a fireman.'

"Pete was the leading firefighter in New York City. He had lectured all over the world on fire science. He was an expert, one of the leading experts in the world. Just a fireman, my butt!

"Pete was a paratrooper in Viet Nam so it seemed he had been groomed to be an American hero long before September 11. He gave up his life in the line of duty and did so without question, without a regard for his own life. I will remain forever proud we could call him "family." The mere mention of his name to strangers whom I have guessed to be a New York firefighter all knew him or heard of his winning ways.

"Even some of my former students, who had received disaster training, left the island to help with the effort with only their hearts to guide them in helping fellow Americans. For all of them, and so many other unheralded heroes in America's wonderful history, I owe them endless appreciation. We all do.'"

We will hear again from the Gantts from their book, "I Gantt Believe Life Is This Good.) She describes her husband and son-in-law's connection with the White House.

September 12, 2007
The White House

"On September 12, Freddie met Vice President Dick Cheney along with Bill Gates. At that event he was presented the Secretary of Defense Employee Support Freedom Award for his efforts about to be explained. One of the Fred's highlights was meeting President George Bush at the White House, a direct result of what Freddie as part of a fifteen-person group had done earlier.

"Freddie described his group:

"' It was made up of some supporters of the local army national guard and reserve unit. The story that led to the group's forming had a family link.'

"When our son-in-law Tim (my cousin) was deployed as a UH-60 Black Hawk helicopter pilot out of the 150th Aviation, Air Assault from Wheeling, he knew there were problems. He was concerned about the distance from the command post to the flight line at Forward Operating Base in Speicher, Iraq. The distance was almost a mile and each person of the four-person crew had to carry 150 pounds of gear, weapons, and ammunition, in 135 degree heat. That effort wore them out before they even left on a mission.

"Tim talked with Janesa (his wife & my daughter) who came to me. I then connected with a couple of fellow businessmen, Bill Newbraugh, Dewey Whitmore and Dan Ryan, friends we've done work for. We raised the $20,000 to buy four Polaris Rangers, the small all-terrain vehicle-style truck called 'gators' which could move the equipment to and from the flight line.

"When Tim was deployed to Iraq from July 2006 to July 2007 his unit flew 200 missions and flew more than 600 hours. Those gators were a godsend, just invaluable.

"Tim added, 'Many times I had members of my unit start trying to express what it was like to have those and they literally couldn't find the words. They were used 24/7. If they weren't supporting crews, they were supporting maintenance.'

"Freddie said, 'We weren't going to make a big deal out of it but Janesa thought otherwise. She nominated our company to receive the prestigious Secretary of Defense Employer Support Freedom Award. Our company was among fifteen businesses selected to receive the yearly award.'

"I feel that we all need to do what we can to help our country. If we don't unite, we fall apart.

"So we were honored on September 12, 2007, for something our country was proud of. I served as the representative of the other fifteen recipients that day. I didn't think it was a particularly big deal, but I guess others did.

"Our government wanted to honor us for making the effort to buy these gators so they took some of us out to Fort Sill to see an operation out there on a C130. They, with the president, the military flew a Blackhawk in here to pick Eric and me up and flew us to Ft. Sill and then on to Wheeling.

"When I met President Bush in the Oval Office the next day on September 13, 2007, I found him most friendly and personable. He was, in no way, a phony. He is the kind of guy I'd like to take fishing. If Gale Catlett (former University of West Virginia basketball coach) and all of us could get together, it would be a ball."

Summer, 2011
Martha's Vineyard

Below is an account from my own life story titled "Hey Jay, What's the Story?"

"Living on the beautiful island of Martha's Vineyard, we get many opportunities twelve months a year to view beautiful sunsets. One of the islanders' favorite sunsets occur over West Chop in the town of Vineyard Haven, at the very northern tip of the triangular-shaped Vineyard.

"During one summer evening in the year 2011, my wife and I anticipated a beautiful sunset about 7 p.m. We took the short drive up to West Chop to watch the sun 'call it for the day.' When we arrived, we were not alone as other islanders were also there to catch the tradition of sunset-watching.

"As we parked our car in our traditional spot on the side of the road we saw about twenty other couples dressed in wedding attire as they came out of the West Chop clubhouse a short distance from the viewing point near the flagpole. Evidently, a wedding celebration was underway and the attendees had the same idea of watching and photographing the beautiful sunset.

"I saw the usual throng of folks but noticed a man who had parked his car, got out, and began taking photos as the sun was just setting. Noticing that he was driving an out-of-state car and seeing his peculiar parking spot I figured he was another summer visitor and one unconnected with the wedding party.

"Something compelled me to get out of our car and approach this man with the express purpose of engaging him in conversation. I did just that beginning with such bland questions as ' . . . beautiful sunset, huh?' He agreed.

"'Are you from here?' I asked.

'He answered, 'No. Actually, I grew up in California and heard all about Martha's Vineyard. I promised myself I'd go there some day. I joined the military early and am now stationed in Alabama. Recently, I got transferred to Connecticut for some advanced training as a Blackhawk helicopter pilot and had a weekend break so decided to check out the Vineyard.'"

"Hearing his Blackhawk helicopter reference and hoping to semi-intelligently carry on the conversation, I offered, 'That's interesting to me as I have a cousin who was also a Blackhawk helicopter pilot who once had an interesting mission in December of 2006. He was assigned to fly Saddam Hussein's dead body from Bagdad to his Al-Awja, near his home town of Tikrit, after the hanging.'

"The man visibly became very interested after I spoke but then looked me in the eye and replied, 'That's interesting. I am the pilot who transported a very alive Saddam Hussein TO his hanging.'

"Immediately, I felt goosebumps forming on my arms and they reappear each time I tell this story years later. What were the chances of that happening that I would know both helicopter pilots involved in the death of Saddam Hussein?

"I could only guess that God had placed me there that late afternoon at sunset time for a reason. He, or something, compelled to leave my car and begin small talk with this perfect stranger. Perhaps our Lord thought it was a neat story and that I'd somehow share a story that only happened to me."

This event is the final entry for "Pearls of Patriotism."

I hope the reader has found that this unique collection of stories from the varying perspectives of my former clients who came to America from all over the world along with those native-born. Based on oral history, these family accounts have been passed down through many generations of appreciative Americans. Whether the voices came from immigrants to America or those born within our borders, their stories have given us a great portrait in print showing America why it is what it is.

I hope you have enjoyed reading this book as much as I enjoyed writing it.

Edwards Brothers Malloy
Thorofare, NJ USA
April 18, 2013